FINDING YOUR PART IN

GOD'S MASTER STORY

ENDORSEMENTS

"If you have ever questioned what you believe, this book is for you! *Finding Your Part in God's Master Story* takes a unique and refreshing approach to the subject of world views. Author, Janet Ruth invites the reader to participate in a journey of discovery. Along the way, you will examine some of your most basic beliefs about God, the world, how things work, and, most importantly, where you fit in. Many books are interesting. Few are worthwhile. *Finding Your Part in God's Master Story* is both."

Dr. Robert L. Edmondson
Author of *It Only Hurts on Monday*,
International Liaison, Global Training Network

"In our post-Christian culture, Janet Ruth offers a study that looks at the overarching themes of faith and the Bible and helps the participant find their voice, place, and story within God's story for humanity. She does this in an accessible way that will deepen the faith journey of any participant."

Dr. Erin Reibel
Christian Speaker and Coach

"Do you find it's hard to walk the talk? When our day to day actions don't reflect our beliefs, is it because we're confused by too many world views bombarding us? Janet Ruth offers this indispensable guide through today's worldviews so we will better understand our place in God's Master Story. The more we know His view and His story, the better we will know and do our part in it."

Elaine Tomski
Award-winning writer, author of *Behind My Bellybutton*,
and contributing writer to *Just Plain Values Magazine*

"Janet Ruth has produced a group study that is wrapped in a unique and effective exterior. It introduces many of the prominent interpretations of varying theological topics in the Bible, and then gives the reader space to think about them, research them, discuss them, and draw their own conclusions. All of this is done in a way that breaks down the more technical aspects of the arguments into easy to understand summaries. Guidance is gently offered where errors occur in interpretation, but room is also given to create and form opinions within the boundaries of the discussion. Overall, this is a study that will open the door for many students of the Bible to dig deeper in their understanding of the Bible and finding answers to life's larger questions."

Dr. Steven Hallam
Associate Professor and Chair of the General Education Department,
Alaska Christian College

"Everyone thinks through it, feels through it, and dreams through it, but too many people don't know what it is, much less develop it and then use it effectively and consistently. This "it" is worldview—the framework, the basic assumptions, the foundational ideas, the lens through which we make sense of and live in the world. In her book *Finding Your Part in God's Master Story*, Janet Ruth provides readers with the tools they need to understand the Christian faith through worldview glasses. This approach will help readers better grasp Christianity, especially its essentials, and gain better ways to work through their own view of Christianity and its application to their lives and beyond. Ruth has provided a potential game-changer. Read it. Use it. Your life will be better for it."

William D. Watkins
Speaker, teacher, and award-winning author of
numerous articles, study guides, and books, including
Worlds Apart: A Handbook on Worldviews and *The New Absolutes*

FINDING YOUR PART IN

GOD'S MASTER STORY

An Exploration
of Christian Worldviews

Janet Ruth

AMBASSADOR INTERNATIONAL
GREENVILLE, SOUTH CAROLINA & BELFAST, NORTHERN IRELAND
www.ambassador-international.com

FINDING YOUR PART IN GOD'S MASTER STORY

An Exploration of Christian Worldviews
©2021 by Janet Ruth
All rights reserved

ISBN: 978-1-64960-070-7
eISBN: 978-1-64960-071-4

Cover Design by Hannah Linder Designs
Interior Typesetting by Dentelle Design

All Scripture quotations, unless noted, are taken from THE HOLY BIBLE, NEW INTERNATIONAL VERSION®, NIV® Copyright © 1973, 1978, 1984, 2011 by Biblica, Inc.® Used by permission. All rights reserved worldwide.

Scripture quotations marked NASB are taken from the NEW AMERICAN STANDARD BIBLE®, Copyright © 1960,1962,1963,1968,1971,1972,1973,1975,1977,1995 by The Lockman Foundation. Used by permission.

Scripture quotations marked KJV are taken from the King James Version.

Scripture quotations marked ESV are taken from the Holy Bible, English Standard Version, ESV® Text Edition: 2016. Copyright © 2001 by Crossway, a publishing ministry of Good News Publishers.

Flower illustration from Vecteezy.com.

AMBASSADOR INTERNATIONAL
Emerald House
411 University Ridge, Suite B14
Greenville, SC 29601
United States
www.ambassador-international.com

AMBASSADOR BOOKS
The Mount
2 Woodstock Link
Belfast, BT6 8DD
Northern Ireland, United Kingdom
www.ambassadormedia.co.uk

The colophon is a trademark of Ambassador, a Christian publishing company.

CONTENTS

ACKNOWLEDGMENTS

This book was inspired by classes I took while working on a master's degree in Biblical Studies. I realize now that I have been studying the topic of Christian worldviews in one way or another for much of my life. I would like to thank all the teachers, pastors, and Bible study leaders I have been privileged to learn from who encouraged me to study God's Word deeply and base my life on it.

I am especially grateful to these wise men who read some or all of the manuscript as it progressed and provided invaluable feedback and assistance: Dr. Robert L. Edmondson, Dr. Steven Hallam, Dr. Ed DeZago, Dr. James D. Patterson, and William D. Watkins. Thank you to all my friends and family who have prayed for me and encouraged me in this work.

Three books had a large influence on the ideas in this book: James Sire's *Naming the Elephant: Worldview as a Concept*; H. Richard Niebuhr's, *Christ & Culture*; and Robert McKee's *Story: Substance, Structure, Style, and the Principles of Screenwriting*. You will see these names pop up quite a bit. Many references are also made to movies and novels to illustrate my points. You will find a complete list of them in the Creative Works Cited section at the end of the book.

I would also like to thank everyone at Ambassador International for their amazing work bringing this book into being.

INTRODUCTION AND INSTRUCTIONS

Nearly everyone can relate to the mixed feelings of fear and anticipation when something they've written is about to be read by someone else. We write papers for our classes and wait with some concern for the teacher to hand them back with comments and a grade. We write texts and emails to friends and family, wondering if they'll really get what we meant to say. We post to our social media accounts, trying to present the best versions of ourselves, the way we want to be seen by the world. But it's rare for anyone to put pen to paper and write about their deepest beliefs and convictions.

In this book, that is exactly what I'm asking you to do.

And I'm asking you to share those deepest beliefs with others in your class or group.

It's a scary thing to do, but it's also an important thing to do. Just like that grade on our papers tells us if we're correctly understanding our lessons, sharing our beliefs with others tests those beliefs so we can throw out what's bad and hold onto what's good.

As a writer, I have belonged to several writing critique groups. In these groups, writers will get together (in person or online) and share something they have written. Members of the group read or listen to each other's work and provide feedback. Most critique groups have rules: Never be insulting. Always start with a positive comment. Offer constructive criticism aimed at making the work better. Be specific. Be supportive.

There are rules for the one sharing their work, as well: Listen to feedback without interrupting. Don't be defensive. Don't argue. In the end, the work is yours, so learn what you can from the critiques and don't worry about the rest.

The rules for sharing what you write in this book are similar:

- Don't be afraid to share. Everyone has their own unique view of things.
- When listening to others share their ideas and beliefs, be supportive. No insults. No eye-rolls. Just remember the Golden Rule and treat others the way you would like to be treated when it's your turn to share.
- It's okay to ask questions to make sure you understand what someone else is saying.
- Listen to feedback without interrupting or arguing.
- Don't assume there is one right answer.
- Be willing to learn.

Your teacher or group leader may want to add some other rules to this list to make your time together more effective. Write those rules here so you don't forget them.

_____

_____

_____

_____

_____

_____

In this book, you will be encountering a wide range of theological issues and Christian teachings, but this is not a book of theology. We'll only be brushing the surface of some very deep issues. I hope you will make an inventory of the subjects you would like to study further after you finish this book. There's a spot in the back for you to jot those down. Then ask your teacher, group leader, or pastor to suggest other books or websites where you can learn more about those subjects. For now, the plan is to look at these issues quickly to identify what you currently believe about each one and to see if these beliefs hold together to form a consistent and coherent foundation for your worldview.

It can be confusing and disconcerting to discover that not everyone agrees with what you believe—even people who, like you, call themselves Christians—even people who go to the same church as you. You will find a wide range of beliefs in this book—some you will agree with and some you definitely won't. As you discuss your beliefs with others in your class or group, you may be introduced to still other beliefs that aren't mentioned in the book. Or you may have some ideas of your own that aren't included here. Don't be afraid to talk about them.

It's a beautiful and dangerous thing to take out an idea and examine it in the bold light of day. But we cannot live our best lives for God if our heads are filled with untested ideas, including half-truths, false assumptions, incorrect teachings, and self-serving philosophies. If you're willing to take a serious look at your own ideas and beliefs—your own worldview—I challenge you to be open and honest as you work through this book.

You won't find a lot of labels in the book. Even though I present a variety of beliefs on different subjects, I rarely label those beliefs as belonging to one particular denomination or school of thought. I don't want us to get distracted by arguing over details about who believes what and miss the bigger point of the book. Most of the descriptions in the book are generalities, meant to give a basic idea of a Christian belief rather than a detailed analysis. It's a starting point for you to build a consistent and comprehensive Christian worldview as you move forward in your Christian walk.

At the end of Chapter 12 is a place for you to write out your personal beliefs about the different subjects we'll explore in the book. You can make notes there as you go through the chapters or wait until you've finished all the chapters before filling out the chart. Your teacher or group leader can tell you if they want you to wait.

Finally, while the book focuses on beliefs, it's important to remember that our beliefs direct our thoughts and our thoughts direct our actions. So, in the end, this is a book about how we should act—what part we should play in God's master story. Before you begin, look up this verse in your favorite Bible translation and write it out below. It's a good verse to memorize and revisit as you work through the rest of the book.

Romans 12:2:

_____

_____

_____

_____

_____

_____

_____

_____

_____

_____

_____

_____

1

WHAT'S YOUR STORY?

When my family bought a new house, we set up one room with game systems, shelves full of DVDs, movie posters on the walls, and a television. Near the door, we hung a whiteboard where we like to write lines from some of our favorite movies:

"Snakes. It had to be snakes."

"Toto, I've a feeling we're not in Kansas anymore."

"This could be the beginning of a beautiful friendship."

"You're a little scary, you know that? Brilliant, but scary."

"Never tell me the odds!"

In another room, on the wall above my computer desk, I've framed the opening lines from some of my favorite books:*

"Once upon a time, a very long time ago now, about last Friday, Winnie-the-Pooh lived in a forest all by himself under the name of Sanders."

"In a hole in the ground there lived a hobbit. Not a nasty, dirty, wet hole, filled with the ends of worms and an oozy smell, nor yet a dry, bare, sandy soil with nothing in it to sit down on or to eat: it was a hobbit hole, and that means comfort."

"It is a truth universally acknowledged, that a single man in possession of a good fortune, must be in want of a wife."

Of course, a single line from a book or movie is not a story in itself. But a memorable line from a well-crafted story has the power to plunge us

---

* If you don't recognize these quotes, turn to the end of the chapter to find out what movies and books they came from.

into the emotional depths of fear, love, anger, joy, and triumph the story originally aroused in us. To this day, my husband has only to say, *"Never trust a bunny,"** to get me to smile—especially when he does it in a high-pitched squirrel voice.

Stories are an integral part of our lives. Every human culture has its stories and storytellers. We tell each other the stories of our lives. We read stories to learn about other cultures and to explore the deeper themes of life and living. We use stories to entertain, but also to teach or to impart wisdom. Jesus loved stories, using dozens of short tales known as parables to teach moral and spiritual lessons. In a world of random, relentless sensory input, we strive to find connections, to see order, to discover the underlying story. It is how we are made—perhaps because we were created by a master storyteller.

There are several important elements that make up a good story: the setting where the story takes place, the characters who move the story forward, the inciting incident, and the climax, to name a few. Those same elements can help us understand the story of God's work in His creation and our own place in it. They can help us define our worldview.

DEFINING WORLDVIEW – THE "MASTER STORY"

When we look beyond our individual situations in life and try to understand our part in the greater story of the world around us, we are exploring what sociologists and psychologists call our *worldview*. Worldview has been defined in many ways, but it is basically the accumulation of what we believe about the existence of God and the nature of reality, the world, and our place in it. It is "the fundamental perspective from which one addresses every issue of life."[1] Each person has a worldview—a collection of beliefs that guides their lives—but few of us take the time to sort through our beliefs to see if they hold together to make a consistent whole.

---

*   If you don't recognize these quotes, turn to the end of the chapter to find out what movies and books they came from.

While the term *worldview* is fairly new, the search for a way to explain our world and our purpose in it isn't new. People throughout history have asked big questions such as: Where did the world come from? Does life have meaning? Is there someone or something in control of our destiny? Attempts to answer those questions led to the development of primary worldviews that answer the big questions in their own way. These include theism (a personal God created and sustains the universe), pantheism (the universe and God are one and the same), deism (God exists beyond the universe but is not active in it), polytheism (there are multiple gods within the universe and active in it), and atheism (there are no gods; the universe was not created and is all that exists).[2]

Some books limit their definition of worldview to include only the primary worldviews, such as those listed above,[3] or they may include other -isms like pluralism, humanism, and relativism.[4] Other writers compare and contrast groups within these primary categories, giving them the name *worldview* as well.[5] For instance, Christianity, Judaism, and Islam can be considered different worldviews in the primary category of theism. But even within these smaller categories, there are many different and conflicting ways people understand our world. When we look deeply enough, we see that we each have our own individual worldview based on what we personally believe. Our personal worldviews are influenced by what we have learned, observed, and experienced throughout our lives. My personal worldview is how I answer the big questions of life—what I truly believe.

Consider the following definition of worldview penned by Christian author James W. Sire:

> A worldview is a commitment, a fundamental orientation of the heart, that can be expressed as a story or in a set of presuppositions (assumptions which may be true, partially true or entirely false) which we hold (consciously or subconsciously, consistently or inconsistently) about the basic constitution of reality, and that provides the very foundation on which we live and move and have our being.[6]

Let's look at that definition closer. A worldview isn't just about the things we say we believe. It's the beliefs we're committed to. The assumptions our beliefs are based on might be true and reliable, or they might be incorrect or just plain wacky. Sometimes we believe something deep inside without even realizing it, and our beliefs won't always be consistent or logical. But—and here's the important part—those beliefs and assumptions we're committed to provide *"the very foundation on which we live and move and have our being."*[7] What we believe about who we are, where we came from, and where we're going directly influences the way we live our lives. That's very important!

BELIEFS AND ACTIONS

To put Sire's statement another way: our beliefs direct our thoughts and our thoughts direct our actions. Let me go back to some of the movie quotes from the beginning of this chapter to illustrate my point.

Snakes. It had to be snakes.
—Indiana Jones in *The Raiders of the Lost Ark*[8]

Near the beginning of the movie, Indiana reacts violently to a harmless pet snake in his friend's plane, exclaiming loudly, *"I hate snakes!"* Jones' action (or overreaction, in this case) tell us something about what he believes: snakes, all snakes, no matter how small and innocent-looking, are extremely dangerous and should be avoided. But later in the movie, Jones drops into a whole roomful of snakes, at least some of which are clearly dangerous. Why? Did he suddenly develop a new belief about snakes? His line, *"It had to be snakes,"* shows us he didn't. But now we can learn something else about what Jones believes—that it was worth risking his life in that snake-filled room to reach a valuable archeological artifact, the lost Ark of the Covenant.

Never tell me the odds!

—Han Solo in *Star Wars: The Empire Strikes Back*[9]

Trying to escape Imperial starships in the Millennium Falcon, Solo reacts defiantly to the suggestion that he is taking too big a risk by flying into an asteroid field. (*"Sir, the possibility of successfully navigating an asteroid field is approximately three thousand seven hundred twenty to one!"*) What was his belief? He believed the odds didn't apply to him—that he was better, smarter, and luckier than the regular people who made up the statistics. In the movie, Solo is proved right. But then, it was a movie, and he was one of the main characters. That changed the odds in his favor. Put a drunk teenager behind the wheel of a car with the same belief that the odds don't apply to him, and the result might be very different.

While it isn't always possible to know what people believe about God, themselves, or the world they live in, their actions often reveal what's going on inside their minds. Sometimes our actions reveal we don't really believe what we say we believe—or even think we believe. Take, for example, the woman who says she believes in a loving God who will take care of all her needs and yet she spends her days in fretful anxiety about every little thing outside her control. Or consider the man who says he believes in Jesus Christ as his Savior and yet he lives with gut-wrenching guilt and despair over his past. Do they really believe what they say they believe?

As Christians, we are encouraged to live according to our beliefs, but that assumes we understand and recognize what we believe. For the most part, we believe what we've been taught—at least until the circumstances of life cause us to question those beliefs, other people we meet introduce conflicting beliefs, or someone tells us we're stupid or old-fashioned for believing things "no one" believes in anymore. It's important, then, to not only know *what* we believe but also *why* we believe it if we want to be secure in our worldview. It is only then that our actions will consistently reflect what we say we believe.

CHRISTIAN WORLDVIEW – ONE OR MANY?

Most of us can say with some certainty where we fit into the primary worldviews. What I believe about the existence and nature of God determines if I am a theist, an atheist, or a pantheist, or if I fit into another primary category. As I get more specific about what I believe about God—how He has communicated with the world and what His purpose is for humanity—I will probably identify with a specific religious or secular worldview, such as Christianity, pluralism, or hedonism. Unfortunately, too many people identify with a particular worldview without ever really thinking about what they believe. Some people call themselves Christians because they attend a Christian church, were baptized as a child, or were born in a "Christian nation," not because they have carefully considered the teachings of Christianity and adopted those beliefs as their own.

So, how can I be sure what I believe fits into the category of a Christian worldview? There are many books on the topic of Christian worldview and Christian beliefs, but, unfortunately, they don't all define Christianity in exactly the same way. That leads us to another question: is there one Christian worldview or are there many? In other words, is there one set of Christian beliefs we all agree on, or are there more than one? Is there one way to live in our world as a Christian, or do we have different ideas about what a Christian life should look like?

After the death and resurrection of Jesus, the new church established by His disciples existed for hundreds of years as a single, mostly unified, religious group. As time passed, some people began to teach new ideas about the nature of God, Jesus, and the Holy Spirit. Church leaders came together in *councils* to determine if these new teachings were consistent with what had been taught by Jesus, the apostles, and the Scriptures. In a series of *creeds* and *canons*, the councils laid out what Christians should believe about important theological issues. They determined what was *orthodox* for Christianity— "conforming to what is generally or traditionally accepted as right or true;

established and approved"[10]—and what was *unorthodox*—"contrary to what is usual, traditional, or accepted."[11]

However, not everyone agreed with the decisions of these councils. Some groups broke away and no longer participated with the rest of the Church. Others were excluded from the Church and no longer considered to be "Christian."

In 1054, a bigger dispute split the churches in half, with both sides— Roman Catholic and Eastern Orthodox—claiming to have the true doctrine about Christianity. In the sixteenth century, another split occurred, leaving the Roman Catholic Church on one side and several new Protestant denominations on the other. Today, there are at least eight major Protestant groups with thousands of individual denominations and associations. Each of these groups has its own set of beliefs about God, the Bible, and what it means to be a Christian.

Today, the Christian community is divided on doctrinal issues, lifestyle issues, church management issues—even what instruments should be played at church and how loud the music should be. Many people leave one church or denomination to go shopping for another which will fit better with their own beliefs, lifestyle, or preferences. They may choose a church based on the popularity of the pastor, the size of the youth group, or certain programs the church offers, without ever asking themselves the most important question: Does this church teach a true Christian worldview?

NOT THE SAME STORY

So, what is a Christian worldview? There are many books on the subject, but they don't all agree on what Christians should believe or how they should act. If you look at the various Christian beliefs about how our world started, what went wrong, what God is doing about it, and where the world is headed, you will see many differences in the master story Christians rely on to understand their world. The question is, are these different ways of seeing the *same* story or are they *different* stories?

As any lover of Shakespeare knows, a good story can be retold and reshaped in a hundred ways. A quick online search will reveal dozens of books and movies based on the ill-fated love story of Shakespeare's *Romeo and Juliet*. There is a difference, though, between retelling a story and making a new story with similar elements. At some point, differences in the main elements of the story—the theme, the characters, or the final resolution—transform a remake into a whole new story. *Romeo and Juliet* would not be *Romeo and Juliet* if the love of two people was not threatened by the very different families or factions of the lovers. Whether the story is called *West Side Story* (1961), *Pizza My Heart* (2005), or even *Gnomeo and Juliet* (2011), the basic plot must remain the same or the story becomes simply "inspired by" or "adapted from" and not the real thing at all.

In the same way, those who claim the name of Christian must share a belief in the same main elements of their worldview. There are many ways to view the story of our world, but very few can legitimately claim to be a Christian worldview.

Through the rest of this book, I will try to help you understand what you believe by exploring a number of Christian worldviews through the viewpoint of their master story. Stories have a beginning, a middle, and an end. They have settings, characters, and themes. They have a plot that takes the main character or characters through a series of conflicts and challenges to a fitting ending. And they have an author. Through each of these elements, we will explore different ways Christians understand God's story and their part in it. We will also see that some teachings which claim to be Christian don't reflect the basic elements of true, biblical Christianity.

God is a master storyteller, and we are part of His story. If we are to understand our place in that story, every part of the story matters—the beginning, the middle, and the end.

YOUR TURN

Before you move on, write out some of your favorite lines from movies or books you have enjoyed. What was it about those stories that made them memorable for you?

_____

_____

_____

_____

_____

_____

_____

_____

_____

_____

_____

CHAPTER CHALLENGE

How many quotes did you recognize from the beginning of this chapter? The movie quotes were from *Indiana Jones: Raiders of the Lost Ark*; *The Wizard of Oz*; *Casablanca*; *Harry Potter and the Sorcerer's Stone*; and *Star Wars Episode V - The Empire Strikes Back*.[12] The book quotes were from A.A. Milne's *Winnie the Pooh*, J.R.R. Tolkien's *The Hobbit*, and Jane Austen's *Pride and Prejudice*.[13] "Never trust a bunny" is a quote from the animated movie *Hoodwinked*.[14]

2

EXPECTATIONS

Before an author begins to write a story, he should know the answers to some important questions: Is this story fiction or non-fiction? What kind of story is it? Who is the audience? That last one is more important than you might realize. If you want to write an effective story, you have to know who you're writing for and what their expectations might be. Cross-genre movies, like *Cowboys & Aliens*, may sound intriguing, but we usually like to know what to expect from a movie or book before we dive in. We expect a romance novel to focus on a couple who fall in love and eventually find a way to be together. We expect a horror flick to have lots of action and suspense to keep us on the edge of our seats. And who hasn't stopped watching a television series because it morphed into a different type of show than we had come to expect and enjoy?

In telling a story, a writer must meet certain expectations. Master screenwriter Robert McKee states that the author "must not only fulfill audience anticipation, or risk their confusion and disappointment, but he must lead their expectations to fresh, unexpected moments, or risk boring them."[15] Authors of non-fiction books also risk confusing and disappointing their readers if they launch into a discussion using terms or ideas the readers don't expect. So, before we move on to consider how various story elements can help us understand our worldviews, let's first consider some different definitions of worldview. Then we'll all know what to expect from the coming chapters.

CHOOSING A FOCUS—EXTERNAL OR INTERNAL

Many people familiar with our topic describe worldview as a list of beliefs, often called *propositions*, shared by the proponents of different faiths or belief systems. The focus is external—on the set of beliefs—rather than internal—on the person who holds them. When the early church fathers created their creeds, they also used a descriptive list as a way to define orthodox Christianity and distinguish it from non-orthodox beliefs. (You can look at the Nicene Creed in the back of this book for an example). There's nothing wrong with that approach to understanding worldviews, but it isn't the only way to explore and understand our beliefs.

Other people look at the idea of worldview as an individual's understanding of the world around him (an internal focus) rather than the list of theological or philosophical propositions the person says he believes (an external focus). In his book on this subject, Christian apologist and lecturer James Sire reviews many different definitions of worldview, some internal and some external. My favorite one is internal, focusing on the heart of the individual rather than the mind:

> A worldview may well be defined as one's comprehensive framework of basic beliefs about things, but our *talk* (confessed beliefs or cognitive claims) is one thing, and our *walk* (operative beliefs) is another and even more important thing. A lived worldview defines one's basic convictions; it defines what one is ready to live and die for.[16]

An internal worldview, then, is a commitment to beliefs deep inside us rather than a list of things we say we believe. When we look carefully at those deeply held beliefs, we find that we don't always *act* as if we believe what we *say* we believe. It's only when we align our internal beliefs with our proclaimed external propositions that our walk will begin to match our talk.

CHOOSING A METHOD—PRESUPPOSITIONS OR STORY

The rest of this book will look at Christian worldviews from an internal perspective. But there is more than one way to explore an internal worldview.

Let's look again at James Sire's definition of worldview from Chapter 1:

> A worldview is a commitment, a fundamental orientation of the heart, that can be expressed as a story or in a set of presuppositions (assumptions which may be true, partially true or entirely false) which we hold (consciously or subconsciously, consistently or inconsistently) about the basic constitution of reality, and that provides the very foundation on which we live and move and have our being.[17]

Sire goes on to explain:

> A worldview is not a story or a set of presuppositions, but it can be expressed in those ways. When I reflect on where I and the whole of the human race have come from or where my life or humanity itself is headed, my worldview is being expressed as a story. Each major worldview has its own metanarrative, its own master story.[18]

Instead of looking at external propositions to define worldview, Sire recommends we look at the beliefs of the individual, focusing on the internal. This can be done by listing our beliefs in a set of presuppositions *or* by exploring the "master story" which explains our world. In this book, we will be exploring our internal worldviews using the elements of storytelling. I hope you will see the advantage of this as we proceed, but first, let's take a closer look at the differences involved in using story rather than presuppositions to explore worldviews.

A presupposition is something we "suppose or assume beforehand;" something we "take for granted in advance."[19] Essentially, it is the things we think we know about the world, ourselves, God, and others. A presupposition may be a belief we rely on because we have investigated it and found it to be reliable, or it could be something we assume is true even though we've never really thought about it. Either way, our presuppositions about the world are the core beliefs which motivate our actions because we act as if they are true—whether they are or not.

For example . . .

"It is a truth universally acknowledged, that a single man in possession of a good fortune, must be in want of a wife."

—Jane Austen's *Pride and Prejudice*[20]

In Jane Austen's novel, Mrs. Bennet believed the most important thing she could do for her daughters was to find them husbands, the richer the better. All of her actions were motivated by this belief, despite her daughter's attempts to convince her that being single was preferable to being married to a stupid, prideful, or selfish man. Her presupposition (deeply held belief) was stronger than her daughter's reasonable arguments, and she acted consistently with her belief.

Can you think of other presuppositions people act on in stories or in real life which may not be true?

_____

_____

_____

_____

_____

_____

The most important thing about our personal worldview is what we believe about God. What we assume, or think we know, about God will affect most of what we do in our lives.

The worldview of an atheist begins with the presupposition that there is no God. His beliefs about the world involve the laws of nature, modified by his own investigation, education, and life experiences. He assumes everything he sees can be explained by those laws, and if he can't explain it, it's only because he hasn't discovered all the facts or isn't aware of all the natural laws. He is much more concerned with using the laws of nature and of mankind for his own benefit than following the laws of some "God" who doesn't exist.

An agnostic begins with the presupposition that it is impossible to know if God exists or not. She rejects the claim of atheism that science proves the lack of any supernatural power, but she also rejects the claims of organized religions that God has revealed Himself and His will to humanity. Many people have no specific beliefs about God, yet they believe in a "cosmic karma" where "what goes around comes around" and "everything balances in the end." They tend to live by their own sense of right and wrong, assuming (consciously or subconsciously) that they will ultimately be judged (by God or the universe) on their general character in life rather than by some objective requirement.

A theistic worldview begins with a belief in the existence of God—one who can be known and who has communicated with the people of this world at different points in history. Theists also believe God ordained certain laws and rules as an objective standard by which all people will be judged. That belief should affect the choices they make and the way they live their lives.

A FOUNDATION FOR CHRISTIAN BELIEFS

When asked about their beliefs, most people will come up with a list of presuppositions which describe their basic understanding of the world. When asked what they believe about God, Christians are likely to refer to things they have learned from the Bible. The Bible tells us many things about who and what God is: "Almighty" (Genesis 17:1); "compassionate and gracious" (Exodus 34:6); "holy" (Leviticus 11:44); "everlasting" (Nehemiah 9:5); "a righteous judge" (Psalm 7:11); and "the King of all the earth" (Psalm 47:7)— just to name a few qualities. It also tells us who we are. We were created by God in His image (Genesis 1:27), but we are mortal (Genesis 6:3), sinful (Romans 3:23), and destined for judgment (Hebrews 9:27).

When asked about how we should live, Christians may also refer to the Bible, where we find many guidelines for living. God gave the Ten Commandments to Moses, along with over 600 other rules and regulations to guide the actions of the nation of Israel. Jesus gave many specific examples of right and wrong behavior in the four Gospels of the New Testament. In other parts of the New Testament, Paul and other apostles provide rules for Christian living and instructions for building up the church.

Although most Christians agree we should rely on the Bible as the foundation for what we believe and how we should act, the Bible is much more than a list of doctrinal statements and rules and regulations. Most of the Bible is written in narrative form—in stories. Even God's laws, like the Ten Commandments, are revealed in the midst of a story of God interacting with His people. They were given at a particular time and to a particular people in unique circumstances. When we take the laws and doctrinal statements out of the context of the stories within the Bible, we miss part of what God is trying to show us.

We can also make some serious mistakes by limiting our beliefs about God to a set of presuppositions. When we use propositions and presuppositions to define who God is, we can forget that the infinite cannot be fully explained in finite words and phrases. We end up putting God in a box of our own making. When we rely on propositions and presuppositions to describe how God wants us to act, making a list of His dos and don'ts for our lives, we may overlook the grander purposes behind the rules. We can forget that, in God's eyes, having the right attitudes and motives may sometimes be more important than following the rules (see Hosea 6:6).

God could have written out a list of very specific rules and said, "Here, do this. This is how I want you to live." But He didn't. He didn't provide us with a theological treatise of all the things He wanted us to know about who He is and what His plan is for His creation. On the other hand, He didn't create us and then sit back to watch from a distance without ever communicating with us at all. God interacted with and spoke to specific people, families, and nations, and had those interactions written down—not strictly in propositions, but largely in narrative form—in stories.

FROM PRESUPPOSITIONS TO MASTER STORY

Many of us were introduced to the Bible through its stories. We learned about Adam and Eve chatting with a snake in an apple tree, Noah filling a boat with animals, David slaying a giant, and Jesus healing the blind and lame. Usually, we look at one story at a time, trying to find a clear lesson about how God wants us to live. We read that Noah was saved because of his faithfulness (Genesis 6), Moses was commended for his humility (Numbers 12), and a blind man was healed because of his faith (Mark 10:46-52), so we try to be like those people. Sometimes the stories we read in the Bible may reveal multiple meanings, like the foreshadowing of Jesus' death seen in the story of the Passover (Exodus 12) or the description of the King of Babylon which is often thought to be a reference to the fall of Satan (Isaiah 14:12-15).

Other Bible stories challenge us and defy understanding, like Jephthah, a leader of Israel who may have killed his daughter after promising to make a burnt sacrifice out of the first thing to come out of his house when he got home from a battle (Judges 11:29-40). What are we supposed to learn from that? Be careful what you promise God? Sometimes it's better not to keep your promises to God? Don't go rushing to greet your father if he has a history of making rash promises to God?

While there is something to learn from every story in the Bible, it's when we put them all together that we begin to understand more about our God, our world, and ourselves than we could ever learn from a list of rules or a theological treatise. We see a God who has been present from the very beginning, a God in action, a God with a purpose. Moreover, we see a God who wants to have a relationship with His people based on trust and love, not just outward obedience (Hosea 6:6; Micah 6:8). That's a lesson that is hard to learn from a list of rules or belief statements but can clearly be seen in the story of God working through His people throughout the Bible.

This doesn't mean we shouldn't be able to state clearly what we believe about God and what He intends for our lives. But getting to know God goes a lot further than being able to recite a list of verses describing His qualities. Living like you believe in God requires a lot more than following a bunch of rules. Understanding your part in His story involves more than joining a church and agreeing with their statement of faith.

In *Experiencing God: Knowing and Doing the Will of God*, theologian Henry Blackaby wrote:

> Scripture is filled with descriptions of God's character. You can read these accounts and believe them to be true about God. Yet God does not merely want you to read *about* Him, He wants you to *know* Him . . . We come to truly know God as we experience Him in and around our lives. Many people have grown up attending church and hearing about God all their lives, but they do not have a personal, dynamic, growing relationship with God. They never hear His voice. They have no idea what God's will is. They do not encounter his love firsthand. They have no sense of divine purpose for their lives. They may know a lot about God, but they don't really know Him.[21]

Examining your personal, internal worldview in light of God's master story can lead you to that place of *knowing* God instead of just knowing about him. Understanding your part in that story will enable you to walk the walk instead of just talking the talk. Are you ready to dig in?

YOUR TURN

Go back to pages 28-29 and read the description of the atheistic, agnostic, and theistic worldviews. List some characters below from movies, television, or books that fit each of these descriptions. Which ones can you relate to?

_____

_____

3

POINT OF VIEW

Once the author has decided what genre her story will be and who her audience is, the next thing she must decide is, "Who is going to tell this story?" It may seem like a silly question. It's the author, of course, who is telling the story when she writes it down. But when writing, the author is usually telling a story about someone else—one main character or maybe a group of people. The author tells the story through them as if it were *their* story. When the writer chooses who will tell the story, she's choosing a *point of view*.

Point of view is the perspective from which a story is told. The story may be told in first person—with a character in the story narrating and using the pronoun *I* to refer to himself. Or the story may be told in third person—with the author narrating and using the pronouns *he, she,* and *they* to refer to all the characters. There are also some second-person stories, where *you* are a character in the story, but these are difficult to write and confusing to read.

In addition to who is telling the story, the author also must decide how much the storyteller knows and can reveal. Older classics, like Jules Verne's *Around the World in Eighty Days*, are told from an *omniscient* point of view—where the narrator tells us what everyone is doing and what everyone is thinking. Today, though, most stories are written in a *limited* point of view—where the narrator tells the story through one character at a time, sharing with the reader only what that character knows, what that character sees and hears, and what that character thinks.

In a first-person narrative, it's easy to recognize who is telling the story. *The Help* is the story of three women living in Mississippi in 1962. A woman named Aibileen begins the story, and we see the world through her eyes:

> Taking care of white babies, that's what I do, along with all the cooking and the cleaning. I done raised seventeen kids in my lifetime. I know how to get them babies to sleep, stop crying, and go in the toilet bowl before they mamas even get out a bed in the morning.[22]

Stories written in third person may be told through one character's perspective or more than one. *Ender's Game* is the story of a young boy raised to become a military leader in an intergalactic war. It is very much Ender's story, even though it's written in third person:

> Endor turned around. He glanced at the men gathered at the back of the room. Most of them he had never seen before. Some were even dressed in civilian clothes. He saw Anderson and wondered what he was doing there, who was taking care of the Battle School if he was gone. He saw Graff and remembered the lake in the woods outside Greensboro, and wanted to go home. Take me home, he said silently to Graff.[23]

Writing from one perspective at a time allows the author to draw the reader into the story so we stand right beside Aibileen or Ender and experience everything happening just as they do. The author of the story knows everything that is happening and what will happen next, but the reader must wait with the characters to see how all will be revealed in the end.

THE BIGGER STORY

When we speak of God's master story, we are talking about a story spanning from creation until the end of time. Some of the story has already been told—in the Bible and the history of the Church and the testimonies of Christians around the world. Our own part of the story is being revealed one day at a time. We can't skip forward a few pages to see what is going to happen to us tomorrow, next week, or next year, but we can know more about our present lives and our future by understanding the bigger story in which we have a part.

One of my favorite scenes from *The Lord of the Rings* series finds Frodo and Sam on the edge of the terrible land of Mordor, trying to find a way in. Remembering the stories of heroes of the past while dealing with their own seemingly impossible situation, Sam suddenly realizes he and Frodo are part of an ongoing story that began long before their time.

> "Don't the great tales never end?"
> "No, they never end as tales," said Frodo. "But the people in them come, and go when their part's ended. Our part will end later— or sooner."[24]

Like Sam, we can find it hard to imagine we're in the same story as great people like Moses, Daniel, Job, Esther, and Peter. It can be hard to believe God has a purpose and role for us like He did for them. Understanding our place— our part of the story—becomes easier when we better understand their parts. Understanding the Bible requires we know how it was written, including— very importantly—the point of view in which the Bible and all its parts were written. There are a variety of thoughts on this issue, but only some can be considered part of a Christian worldview.

A LIMITED POINT OF VIEW: THE BIBLE WAS WRITTEN BY HUMANS

For the non-Christian, it is easy to believe the Bible is a collection of books written, edited, and collected by humans for human purposes. Some believe it to be a book about being moral, or an attempt to create a history for the Jewish people, or even that it was written by first century Christians to undermine the Roman Empire. Most of the book is believed by non-Christians to be fiction, written long after any real events occurred, with made-up events (like the creation account, the flood, and the miracles of Jesus) thrown in to make a better story.

Even some people who call themselves Christians believe the Bible is largely fiction. They believe the events written about either didn't happen at all or they were written down by people who weren't there but were merely recording tales passed down for generations. Some believe God is not revealed primarily through the Bible but through their own personal experiences with God, and they are free to take from the Bible whatever suits their own feelings.

Others believe the Bible is mostly true, and the events it records really happened in one form or another, but the stories are told strictly through the perspective of the various writers. This allows for a belief in God as He is described in the Bible, but it also allows a way to question the literal truthfulness of the Bible. Human authors, writing without the direct revelation of God, make human mistakes. They write with human biases, with the limitations of a particular human culture, and for a particular time. This viewpoint allows each reader of the Bible to choose what they will believe about the Bible and what they can ignore.

AN OMNISCIENT POINT OF VIEW: THE BIBLE WAS WRITTEN BY GOD

A very different belief is that the Bible was inspired directly by God through the Holy Spirit and is entirely His revelation about Himself in His own words. The Bible itself claims that God was involved in its writing: "For prophecy never had its origin in the human will, but prophets, though human, spoke from God as they were carried along by the Holy Spirit"; "For all Scripture is God-breathed and is useful for teaching, rebuking, correcting and training in righteousness" (2 Peter 1:21; 2 Timothy 3:16). Other translations of 2 Timothy 3:16 say that scripture is "inspired by God" (NASB), "given by inspiration of God" (KJV), or "breathed out by God" (ESV).

John R.W. Stott, Anglican priest and theologian, writes about the profound nature of inspiration:

> *Inspiration* indicates the chief mode God has chosen by which to
> reveal himself . . . We do not use it in the general sense that we

may say a poet or musician is "inspired." On the contrary, it has a special and precise connotation, namely that "all Scripture is God-breathed" (2 Timothy 3:16). . . . The meaning, then, is not that God breathed into the writers, nor that he somehow breathed into the writings to give them their special character, but that what was written by human authors was breathed out by God. He spoke through them. They were his spokesmen.[25]

The benefit of this belief is that it gives authority to the teachings of the Bible because it is God's Word—an authority missing from a collection of works by unaided human authors. Someone who believes in the Bible as God's Word can have confidence in knowing God as He has revealed Himself. Some of the challenges with this belief include trying to explain apparent inconsistencies in the text, dealing with claims of "impossibilities" (such as the accounts of creation and the flood), and having to live by a strict moral code that feels out of place in modern societies.

COMBINING THE TWO: THE BIBLE WAS WRITTEN BY GOD THROUGH A HUMAN PERSPECTIVE

In between these two positions is the idea that God partnered with humans to write the Bible through the words and perspectives of the human writers. Like Aibileen, Minny, and Miss Skeeter in *The Help*, each of the writers of the books of the Bible had their own limited viewpoint from which to tell their story and their own style. But through the various individual stories, the message of God as the author shows through.

Charles C. Ryrie explains the inspiration of the Bible like this:

> God superintended the human authors of the Bible so that they composed and recorded without error His message to mankind in the words of their original writings . . . The word "superintended" allows for the spectrum of relationships God has with the writers and the variety of material. His superintendence was sometimes very direct and sometimes less so, but always it included guarding the writers so that they wrote accurately.[26]

Some writers in the Bible wrote in first person about their own experiences, like Zechariah the prophet:

> During the night I had a vision, and there before me was a man mounted on a red horse. He was standing among the myrtle trees in a ravine. Behind him were red, brown and white horses. I asked, "What are these, my lord?" (Zechariah 1:8-9).

Others wrote in third person about the experiences of others:

> After the death of Joshua, the Israelites asked the Lord, "Who of us is to go up first to fight against the Canaanites?" (Judges 1:1).

Many recorded not only their own thoughts and actions but the very words of God:

> Therefore this is what the Lord says: "I will return to Jerusalem with mercy, and there my house will be rebuilt. And the measuring line will be stretched out over Jerusalem," declares the Lord Almighty (Zechariah 1:16).

> The Lord answered, "Judah shall go up; I have given the land into their hands" (Judges 1:2).

Some wrote using approximations and hyperbole (exaggerations not meant to be taken literally). Some used idioms, such as the "four corners of the earth" mentioned in Revelation 7:1. Different authors gave different descriptions of the same events, even the same quotation, revealing what the author thought was important about that event or statement.

The advantage of this belief is that it still recognizes the authority of the Bible as God's Word, but it frees the reader from accepting every word in its most literal sense. The disadvantage is that it requires us to carefully study the Bible to understand the truths which God, the author, is revealing through the stories written by human hands.

These are only three viewpoints about the Bible, and they are rather general in nature. You may have heard other ideas about who wrote the Bible or the reason it was written. As we go on, I think it will become clear how very important this core belief is as part of your worldview. It is tempting to disregard parts of the Bible we don't understand or don't want to believe are true. It is better, though, to study the Bible carefully and consider different explanations for the sometimes confusing things we read. Only then can we begin to understand the story God is telling in His own words or through the words of human writers.

Before we go on, consider the following two statements and mark on the line where you are right now.

I believe the Bible is God's Word and is true.

_____

0%   100%

I consider the Bible to be authoritative in my life.

_____

0%   100%

YOUR WORLDVIEW—YOUR POINT OF VIEW

How we view the Bible is one of the most important things which will shape our worldview as Christians. But it goes deeper than saying, "I believe the Bible is true" or "I try to obey what the Bible teaches." We have to learn as much as we can about the Bible, think seriously about what it is teaching, and then apply those teachings to our lives. Agreeing to an external set of propositions about the Bible, God, Jesus, etc. won't affect your life nearly as much as internalizing those beliefs and making them truly your own.

In the last chapter, I explained that we would be looking at Christian worldviews from an internal focus rather than external. In terms of point of view, my worldview is *my* story understood from my own perspective. It is based on what I see and hear, what I think, and what I believe. Your worldview is *your* story understood from your perspective. It is the accumulation of deep thoughts and attitudes that motivate your actions and give life to your hopes and fears, the way you view yourself, and your ability to relate to others. Stories about other people (real or fictional) can help us understand the world through their experiences, but, in the end, you can only see the world through your perspective, and I can only see through mine.

To understand the deep thoughts and attitudes which make up your own worldview, you need to uncover them and bring them out into the light to look at them. That's not always an easy thing to do, but we must start somewhere. In addition to what we believe about the Bible, there are two fundamental questions which shape our personal worldviews and our identity as Christians.

Consider these two statements, and mark on the lines where you fit. You may be tempted to answer quickly with a high level of confidence in your answers but take some time to consider each question and try to rate yourself *honestly* on a scale of 0 to 100 percent. While it may be difficult to be truthful about what you really believe, it's the first step you must take in understanding your worldview.

I believe God exists.

_____

0%   100%

I think we can agree that someone who doesn't believe in God at all is not a Christian, but not all people who think of themselves as Christians are 100% sure God exists. A study released in 2015 revealed that three percent of "religiously affiliated" people in America don't strongly believe in the existence of God.[27] A different study in 2016 showed ten percent of "practicing Christians" didn't agree that there is only one God.[28] This is a clear departure from the earliest creeds, which begin with a declaration of the existence of "one God, the Father, the Almighty, maker of heaven and earth, of all that is, seen and unseen."[29]

I believe that Jesus is the Son of God and the Christ (Savior/Redeemer/Messiah).

0%   100%

People from many religions believe there is a God, but to be a Christian requires a belief in Jesus as well—not just as a person who lived long ago and was written about in the Bible, but as the Son of God who plays a role in our lives as the Savior, Redeemer, or Messiah. Paul called his teachings about Jesus "the gospel" and said, "by this gospel you are saved" (1 Corinthians 15:1-2). Read through the Nicene Creed in the back of this book to see how the early Christians described Jesus. For now, you can ignore any parts you don't understand. Of the parts you do understand, how much do you agree with?

How you answered these questions reveals what you believe *about* God and Jesus, but it doesn't necessarily reveal what you believe *in*. The higher you marked your level of belief, the more likely it is that you are committed to these beliefs and that they form an important part of your personal worldview. However, intellectual belief, no matter how strong, is not enough. You must also learn to trust *in* those beliefs and live like you really believe what you say you believe.

If you aren't fully relying on these beliefs, what's stopping you? Are you a new Christian who still has a lot to learn about what the Bible teaches? Do you have doubts about what the Bible teaches because of what you've learned about scientific discoveries or the beliefs of other worldviews? Or have you simply failed to really think about what you believe and whether it's consistent with a Christian worldview?

To take an external worldview like Christianity and make it part of our personal worldview—those deeply-held beliefs which direct our thoughts and actions—we must understand where we personally fit into the bigger story. Instead of focusing on the story of *my* life and trying to decide how Christianity fits *my* storyline, I need to understand the bigger story—God's Master Story—and look for my place in *His* storyline.

In the rest of this book, I will help you see your story in light of something greater than yourself. You will find yourself within a bigger story—one whose beginning and end stretch far beyond your own. The better you understand that story—God's story—the better you will understand God's role for you in the story of your own life.

YOUR TURN

Before we move past the *you* part of your worldview, think about your own life story for a moment. If a close friend were asked to write your story, what would they say about you? Is there enough evidence from the things you say and do to make it clear to others what you believe about God, Jesus, and the Bible? Should there be?

Write the first paragraph of the story of *you* from your own point of view (first person) or the perspective of a friend (third person). The story can start anywhere—at your birth, a big moment in your life, or maybe even how you came to be in a class or group studying this book. Just write about *you* in your own words or the imagined words of a friend.

_____

_____

_____

_____

_____

4

SETTING

As a story is told, one of the first things we discover is its setting. The *setting* of a story is the time and place in which the characters live and the action occurs. Every story has a setting, and in large or small part it defines the story. The setting of a story can include physical terrain, buildings and cities, the way a home is decorated, historical events, social conditions, weather, and so much more. In some stories, the setting may seem to be nothing but a backdrop, like a painted set piece for a play. But if we look closely, it can reveal information about the characters, move the story forward, or even become a character of the story, such as the harsh Canadian wilderness in Jack London's novel, *The Call of the Wild*.

Just listen to Suzanne Collins set the mood for her best-selling young adult novel, *The Hunger Games*, only six paragraphs into the book, by describing the setting of the heroine's home:

> Our part of District 12, nicknamed the Seam, is usually crawling with coal miners heading out to the morning shift at this hour. Men and women with hunched shoulders, swollen knuckles, many who have long since stopped trying to scrub the coal dust out of their broken nails, the lines of their sunken faces. But today the black cinder streets are empty. Shutters on the squat grey houses are closed. The reaping isn't until two. May as well sleep in. If you can.[30]

Without knowing anything else about this book, you already know something about the main character, Katniss. The place she comes from is bleak, joyless, and full of hardworking but defeated people. We soon come to realize Katniss is also bleak, joyless, and hardworking. Whether she too will be defeated by her circumstances is something the reader will be anxious to find out.

See if you can identify the following films from a brief description of their settings.* What do the different settings tell you about the main characters in those stories?

1. A farm outside a small midwestern town in 1930's America, then a colorful new world where scarecrows, tin men, and lions talk.
2. A city in French-controlled Morocco during World War II with a bar owned by an American ex-patriot.
3. "A long time ago, in a galaxy far, far away."
4. A child's bedroom decorated in a western theme in the beginning but later changed to a space theme. (Hint: this one is an animated film.)

THE HEAVENS AND THE EARTH

In the last chapter, we were reminded that our personal worldview is part of a bigger story. As with most stories, there is more than one setting in God's master story. It encompasses all of time, every nation on our planet, the universe around us, and more.

The very first words of the Bible introduce one setting of the master story: "In the beginning, God created the heavens and the earth" (Genesis 1:1). We have a time, "in the beginning," and we have a place, "the heavens and the earth." Later in this book, we'll look at what is meant by "in the beginning," but for now let's focus on the physical setting described in this verse.

---

* The answers can be found at the end of the chapter.

"The earth" is easy enough to understand. We live here. We know what it looks like and feels like. Science tells us a good deal about how it works. Each one of us lives in a particular place on the earth, and that place affects our personal story, but I think we can agree that God's master story involves the people of the whole earth (see Acts 17:24-28). The cultural aspects of our world have changed dramatically over time as science and technology have evolved and civilizations have come and gone. Even the earth itself—mountains, seas, plants, and animals—has gone through changes since humans first appeared on it. But we still have a good idea of what is described as "the earth" in Genesis 1:1.

What about "the heavens" God created? This could be a reference to the rest of the physical universe beyond planet Earth—the sun, moon, stars, and planets. Although the rest of the universe plays only a small part in the Bible, it tells us something about the God who created it: "The heavens declare the glory of God; the skies proclaim the work of his hands"; "For since the creation of the world God's invisible qualities— his eternal power and divine nature—have been clearly seen, being understood from what has been made, so that people are without excuse" (Psalm 19:1; Romans 1:20).

What about what we cannot see? Did God create a "Heaven" for His own dwelling place in addition to the "heavens" we see? Is "Heaven" a separate place from our universe, or is it a spiritual dimension within the universe? In other words, is God here, all around us, or out there in a distant heavenly city? Or could it be both? While the Bible gives us a few glimpses of God in His dwelling place, it's skimpy on the details. Paul mentions "the heavenly realms" five times in the book of Ephesians, but he never gives us a definition or description of the place (verses 1:3, 1:20, 2:6, 3:10, and 6:12).

Have you ever thought about where God was *before* He created the heavens and the earth? What was His home like then? Just as with Katniss in *The Hunger Games*, what we know (or believe) about a person's home can tell us a lot about that person. Stop for a moment and draw a picture or write out a description of God in His home as you see it:

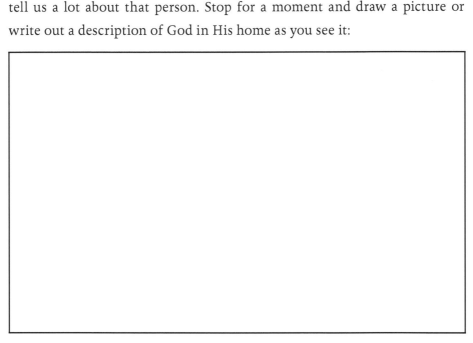

A NEW HEAVEN AND A NEW EARTH

As we move past the first verses and chapters of the Bible, we quickly see a change in the setting. When the work of creation was done, the Bible tells us the earth and all it contained were "very good" (Genesis 1:31). Then sin entered the world and everything changed. The earth became a place where thorns grew and the sun beat down hard on a farmer's back (Genesis 3:17-19). Floods, droughts, diseases, and wild animals threatened mankind. Although not all Christians believe in a literal six-day creation of our world or the existence of Adam and Eve, there is a general consensus that something changed from the way our world began to the way it is today. We'll talk about that more later, but first let's look at the last setting in God's master story.

From the first chapters of the first book of the Bible, we turn to the last chapters of the last book of the Bible:

> Then I saw "a new heaven and a new earth," for the first heaven and the first earth had passed away, and there was no longer any

sea. I saw the Holy City, the new Jerusalem, coming down out of heaven from God, prepared as a bride beautifully dressed for her husband. And I heard a loud voice from the throne saying, "Look! God's dwelling place is now among the people, and he will dwell with them. They will be his people, and God himself will be with them and be their God. 'He will wipe every tear from their eyes. There will be no more death' or mourning or crying or pain, for the old order of things has passed away."

He who was seated on the throne said, "I am making everything new!" Then he said, "Write this down, for these words are trustworthy and true." (Revelation 21:1-5)

Clearly, we have a new setting here, but, again, the details about this place are vague. Is this our existing world changed and perfected by a supernatural act? Is it our world gradually transformed by the work of the Holy Spirit and God's people back to God's original design? Or is it an entirely new setting, a new creation—either physical or spiritual—which replaces the old, hopelessly broken creation we live in now?

Many Christians wonder if it even matters. They may be overwhelmed and mystified by the book of Revelation, or they may agree with scholars who believe Revelation has nothing to do with the future but was written about the persecution of Christians under the Roman Empire of the first century. We'll talk about these ideas more in later chapters, but I want to stress that what we believe about our future does matter. What we believe about how our world started and how it will end influences what we believe about our purpose in the world. It forms two important settings for God's master story and helps us understand the setting we find ourselves in today.

BETWEEN THE BEGINNING AND THE END

Some Christian writers have tried to help us understand the different ways we can view our present setting. In his book, *Christ and Culture*, H. Richard Niebuhr identified five types of Christians based on the way they view the connection between Christ and—you guessed it—culture. By "Christ," Niebuhr meant our understanding of Jesus Christ as the authority for our life choices. In using the term "culture," Niebuhr meant "the 'artificial, secondary environment' which man superimposes on the natural. It comprises language, habits, ideas, beliefs, customs, social organization, inherited artifacts, technical processes, and values."[31] In other words, *culture* for Niebuhr is the setting of the story in which we live, while *Christ* represents a way of thinking about the world and living in it (our worldview).

Niebuhr identified five different ways Christians can view their world by examining what they believe Christ's purpose is for them in relation to their culture. He pointed out more than once in his book that these five viewpoints, or Christian types, as he calls them, are generalizations, and it's possible for someone to relate to more than one of the types or to be unsure of where they fit. The types are useful, though, in understanding how our view of the world around us—our culture, the setting of our story—affects what we believe and how we act.

Christ Against Culture: Niebuhr begins with a type of Christian who believes the world is basically bad. The culture of music, science, entertainment, politics, even education, is permeated with evil. Christians who see the world this way reject their culture and interact with it as little as possible. This thinking can best be seen in the lives of medieval monks who shut themselves up in austere monasteries, but it can also be seen in groups such as the Amish, who live apart from the modern world, or in families who homeschool their children, watch only Christian movies, and live by a strict set of rules set down by the Bible, even when those rules conflict with cultural norms.

Christ Of Culture: The second type is very different from the first, finding much of value in their culture. According to Niebuhr, "They find no great tension between church and world . . . [T]hey understand Christ through culture, selecting from his teaching and action as well as from the Christian doctrine about him such points as seem to agree with what is best in civilization."[32] This attitude was seen in the early days of the church by those who tried to harmonize Christian teachings with Greek philosophies, and it is seen today in denominations which embrace social change by regarding some teachings of the Bible as belonging to another place and time (such as limits on women in leadership and prohibitions on same-sex unions).

Christ Above Culture: Between the two extremes of choosing to live outside our culture or fully in it are three other types of Christians, beginning with the *synthesis* type. This type sees God and His purposes revealed through both the Bible and human reason. They believe God created and maintains culture, so culture is neither good nor bad. Christians, primarily through the institution of the church, are given the task of supervising culture for its own good. "Beyond the state is the church, which . . . as custodian of the divine law assists in the ordering of the temporal life . . . "[33] This type was best expressed in the Roman Catholic Church during the medieval age when the church aligned itself closely with the governments of Europe, influencing all aspects of the culture. Today, it is seen in those whose goal is to see their governments and culture lined up with the teachings of the Bible.

Christ and Culture in Paradox: The second group finding themselves in the middle of the Christ and Culture debate is called the *dualist* type. They try to find a balance between "loyalty to Christ and responsibility for culture."[34] Unlike the *synthesis* type, the *dualists* find difficulty in this balancing act because of the pervasive nature of sin in culture. This type emphasizes the need for the transforming power of God's grace in the lives of individuals through faith in Jesus Christ, without which no lasting spiritual change (in individuals or in culture) can take place. Paul the Apostle and Martin Luther best express the views of this type. Many evangelicals will say they agree with the teachings of this type, but they may look more like the *synthesists* or the *conversionists* in their actions.

Christ the Transformer of Culture: The final type, the *conversionists*, have a hopeful view toward culture, seeing it as God's good creation, marred by sin, but capable of becoming good again through the ongoing work of God in all our lives. They see God already at work making all things new, rather than looking forward to a future transformation. Augustine expressed this view during the last days of the Roman Empire, and the theme was taken up again by John Calvin during the Protestant Reformation in the sixteenth century. It is the view expressed by many Christians today who follow the Reformed tradition.

GOOD, BAD, OR INDIFFERENT?

Perhaps you quickly identified with one of Niebuhr's Christian types, or you saw other people you know in the descriptions. Perhaps this is the first time you stopped to think about your world and how God sees it. I won't ask you to commit to a lifelong belief here, but right now which of the following statements best describes how you view the world you live in?

[ ] The world is inherently bad, stained by sin. People are basically evil. Human institutions (such as governments and public education) are flawed. "Worldly" attitudes seen in non-Christian entertainment, advertising, and consumerism are opposed to God's desires for us.

[ ] The world is good the way it is. God created a good world and gave us the ability to use our minds and abilities to make it even better. People are basically good, and they are capable of improving. Education and good government are essential to making a better world.

[ ] The world is neither good nor bad, though it is affected by the consequences of sin. Christians have a duty to guide and protect cultural institutions like government and education, ensuring that they reflect godly, moral principles.

[ ] The world is both good and bad. There is much that reflects the majesty of the Creator in nature, people, and human institutions, but

all these things are also marred by sin and our separation from God. While we cannot ultimately change the world for the better, we can change lives by sharing the gospel and bringing light to the darkness through our good actions.

[ ] The world has been affected by sin, but it was made to be good and can be good again. Christians should engage with their culture and, with God's power, can help to transform it by intentionally living out their Christian beliefs.

As I stated earlier, the setting of a story in large or small part defines the story. That is true of worldviews as well. As you looked through the options above, I hope you could see how your view of your world (your setting) influences the way you live as a Christian.

Another way to look at our settings is to think of the role they play in a story. So, I'm going to give you another set of options to choose from. In God's master story, which description best describes the setting around us (both the physical world and the culture we live in)?

[ ] It's just a backdrop to the action taking place. It isn't important to the story.

[ ] It's an antagonist, creating conflict the characters in the story must overcome.

[ ] It's the victim of the story, needing help from the main characters to restore it to its intended state.

YOUR TURN

I hope I didn't stress you out too much with this chapter. There isn't one correct answer to any of these questions. Whatever you answered, you will find some Christians who agree with you and others who disagree. The point of the questions is to help you understand what you believe about the world you live in.

You already drew a picture or wrote a description of God's home. Before you move on to the next chapter, draw a picture or write a description of your home—your world—as you think God sees it:

THE CHAPTER CHALLENGE

On page 48, could you identify the movies from their settings? In order, the movies are *The Wizard of Oz, Casablanca, Star Wars: A New Hope,* and *Toy Story.*

5

CHARACTERS

Conflict and change are essential elements of any story. There is movement in a story, sometimes toward a goal and sometimes away from it, and it is the *characters* in the story who create that movement. Characters create conflict with one another, and they react to those conflicts, attempting to change their circumstances and often being changed themselves. Each choice a character is forced to make in a movie or book reveals something about that character—their inner strengths and weaknesses, their hopes and dreams, their loyalties, and their beliefs.

Depending on its genre and length, a story may have many characters, just a few, or even one. Most stories will have main characters, minor characters, and background characters. Background characters are little more than faces in a crowd, and we never learn much, if anything, about them. Major and minor characters have unique qualities, such as race, gender, age, and other physical characteristics, as well as occupations, life experiences, and opinions. The main characters will include the protagonist (the hero) and usually an antagonist (the bad guy). The more important the character is to the story, the more they move the story forward and the more we will learn about that character.

Think of the main character from a book or movie you like and describe them here:

Gender:_____ Race:_____ Age: _____

How they look: _____

What they do: _____

What they are like: _____

_____

One thing every main character needs is motivation. There is something they want or need, and that motivation will become the goal of the story itself. The goal may be to survive a catastrophe (*The Poseidon Adventure*), to find a soulmate (*Serendipity*), or to save the world from an alien invasion (*The Avengers*). Sometimes the goal is very focused, as in *Die Hard*, where a lone police detective must save a group of hostages being held by terrorists on the 30th floor of an office building. Very often, though, a character will have multiple goals, such as Maverick striving to win a competition, get the girl, and distance himself from his father's reputation in *Top Gun*. As each story progresses, goals are achieved, forsaken, or crushed—but in the end, something has changed. Without change, there is no story. And without characters working toward one goal or another, there is no change.

Write the main goal of the character you described above: _____

_____

_____

_____

MOVING THE STORY FORWARD

The word *characters* usually refers to fictional people, but there are characters in true stories as well. When we express our worldview as a story, we find characters there, too.

To understand the master story of your worldview, it's important to identify who you believe is moving the story forward. Who are the main characters who are making things happen, and what are their goals? In later chapters, we'll talk more about these goals and how they affect the action of the story, but for now, take a few moments to consider the *characters* we find in different Christian worldviews.

GOD

One of the earliest creeds of the Christian church states: "We believe in one God, the Father . . . and in our Lord Jesus Christ . . . and in the Holy Spirit."[35] All mainstream Christian groups believe in a Triune God—the Father, Son, and Holy Spirit being three distinct persons sharing one substance or essence as God.[36]

God the Father, Jesus Christ, and the Holy Spirit are all mentioned in the Bible, and we can read there about the role each one has played in the past. But what about now? What about the future? In the master story of where this world came from and where it's going, how should we classify God the Father, Jesus Christ, and the Holy Spirit? Are they main characters (each with a goal they are actively working to achieve), minor characters (helping the main characters achieve their goals), background characters (doing little of importance), or non-existent? In the chart below, indicate with a **T** what your church or denomination teaches about God the Father, Jesus Christ, and the Holy Spirit. You may want to look at your church's doctrinal statement to answer these questions, or you can use the Nicene Creed in the appendix of this book and ask yourself what it teaches.

	Main Character	Minor Character	Background Character	Doesn't Exist
God the Father				
Jesus				
The Holy Spirit				

In your own life, do you believe one or all of these characters are actively working to move you forward toward some goal? Go back and mark with a **B** what roles you believe God, Jesus, and the Holy Spirit play in your personal life story.

SATAN

Every story needs a protagonist—one or more people moving toward a goal. Most stories also have an antagonist—one or more people working to frustrate the protagonist and keep the goal out of reach. In the Bible, we read about Satan (Mark 1:13), the devil (1 Peter 5:8), and the evil one (John 17:15), who are usually considered to be the same person—a spiritual being who rebelled against God and initiated the first sin of human-kind (Genesis 3). However, not everyone believes in Satan. For those who don't believe God wrote or inspired the Bible, it's easy enough to think Satan is just a myth created by the Jews or early Christians to explain the evil they saw in the world. Even some who believe in the Bible as God's inspired Word think of Satan as a metaphor for evil rather than an actual spiritual being.

It may be hard to discover what your denomination believes about Satan. Many doctrinal statements and even books on theology fail to mention him, and many churches avoid the subject in sermons and lessons. To the best of your knowledge, indicate with a **T** what your church or denomination teaches about Satan. Is he a main character in world events, a minor character, a background character, or non-existent? Then indicate with a **B** what you believe about the role of Satan in your own life.

	Main Character	Minor Character	Background Character	Doesn't Exist
Satan				

ANGELS AND DEMONS

Like Satan, angels and demons can be relegated to the realms of myth or metaphor, or they can be seen as real spiritual beings who had roles to play in the Bible and who may, or may not, be active in the world today. Most mainstream churches teach little about these spiritual beings, but individual Christians can become fascinated by them and build up beliefs about demonic or angelic activities based more on their own experiences and ideas than on the teachings of the Bible.

To the best of your knowledge, indicate with a **T** what your church or denomination teaches about angels and demons. Then indicate with a **B** what you believe about their role in your life.

	Main Character	Minor Character	Background Character	Don't Exist
Angels				
Demons				

SAINTS

The Bible refers to all who follow Jesus as "saints," which means "holy ones," but the term has a particular meaning for Catholics. The Roman Catholic Church teaches that all Christians share a "communion of the saints" on earth which continues in heaven. Christians in heaven can intercede and mediate for Christians on earth, sharing in the work of Jesus as part of the "body of Christ." According to the Catholic Church, everyone currently living in heaven is a saint, but not everyone goes immediately to heaven after death. Deceased Christians can be "canonized" by the Church if there "is proof of miracles performed by the deceased Christian after his death," and this confirms that they are, in fact, in heaven.[37] Catholics pray to the saints for intercession, protection, healing, or even to find lost items.

Using this definition of deceased Christians living in heaven, mark a **T** for what your church teaches about saints, and a **B** for what you believe.

	Main Character	Minor Character	Background Character	Don't Exist
Saints				

THE CHURCH

While there are many churches in our world, there is one Church—the community of all believers. The Church is defined in the Bible as the body of Jesus Christ, who is the head of the Church (Ephesians 1:22-23; 1 Corinthians 12:27). One theologian describes the Church as "God's spiritual family, the Christian fellowship created by the Holy Spirit through the testimony to God's mighty acts in Christ Jesus."[38] Many Christians would agree that the purpose of the Church is to carry out the work of God, Jesus, and the Holy Spirit in our world. However, many churches focus on their own small part in reaching this goal without giving much attention to the work of the worldwide Church.

Based on specific teachings, or the lack thereof, what do you think your church believes about the role of the Church in God's master story? What do you believe about the role of the Church in your own life? Use a **T** to mark what your church teaches and a **B** to mark what you believe.

	Main Character	Minor Character	Background Character	Doesn't Exist
The Church				

THE REST OF THE WORLD

A person is either a Christian or they aren't. They are either in the Church or outside it. For more traditional Christians, there is a clear line between Christians and non-Christians, although not all agree on what is required to be "in" rather than "out" of the people of God. There is also disagreement on what will happen eventually for those who are "out."

As stated in the last chapter, some see our human world as being opposed to God, actively disobeying Him and trying to thwart His plans. Others see those outside the Church as victims of a spiritual war they don't understand, and the mission of the Church is to save them. Still others believe the mission of the Church is to redeem God's creation, reforming it into God's original design. They see creation itself as the victim, and mankind can either stand in the way of that reformation or they can aid it, even if they don't realize they are doing God's work.

We'll get to the goal of God's master story in a later chapter, but for now, mark with a **B** what you believe about the role of non-Christians in that story. If you know what your church teaches on these matters, mark that with a **T** as well. Then mark with a **B** and a **T** what you think about the role of God's physical creation and what your church teaches. [Note that the categories are different here.]

	Antagonist	Victim	Minor Character	Background Character
Non-Christians				
Physical Creation				

THE CHOICES WE MAKE

Earlier in this chapter, I said that we learn about characters through the choices they make. But who is really making those choices? In a non-fiction story, the author does his best to write down what a real person did and said and thought. But if the story you're reading is fiction, the author created the characters in the story and decided how each one would act, what they would say, and what would happen to them.

Fiction authors have different ways of making up these characters. Some will use an elaborate system to define each major and minor character, listing their characteristics and personal history in detail before the author even begins writing the story. Others will have a general idea of what a character should be like when they start writing, and with each new situation they let the character "choose" their actions based on what the author feels is right for that character at that moment.

As the characters and plot develop, an author might change the direction of the story to work in new ideas or work out unforeseen difficulties. But eventually, the author's work is done. When you pick up a book to read, the characters and plot are fixed on the pages, and they aren't going to change, no matter how much you may want them to. They can't be read out of the book like the characters of *Inkheart* to make new choices for themselves.

Christians who believe in an eternal God who created us often struggle to understand how much God controls us and how much freedom we have to make our own choices.

In the Bible, David sang to God, "All the days ordained for me were written in your book before one of them came to be" (Psalm 139:16). This idea that God knows everything which has happened, is happening, and will happen is repeated several times in the Bible, and it can be perplexing for Christians. Has God already decided everything that will happen, like the writer of a book, and are we merely characters on a page with no ability to affect our fate? Or does God see the future and know what we will do, even though we freely choose our own actions?

This question of free will versus God's sovereignty has been debated for centuries. Some Christians believe God has absolute knowledge *and control* of the past, present, and future, while others talk about God as if He were running around trying to fix the mess humans created by choosing their own path instead of His will. Some believe God is in ultimate control, but He gives us the freedom to make choices and live according to His will or according to our own. Still others believe humans have been granted great power and responsibility to affect the course of history.

It's not an issue we can resolve today, but it does raise another question you can answer. What do you believe about *your* role in God's master story? Does God have a part for you to play in achieving His goals in this world? Are you capable of making a difference? Are you willing to try? Are you living like you have a part in God's story, or do you treat God like a minor character in *your* life story, there only to help you achieve your goals?

Here's the last table for you to complete. In the first box, add your own name, then mark with a **B** what you honestly believe about your role in God's master story.

	Main Character	Minor Character	Background Character	Don't Know

6

EXPOSITION

I love movies about making movies. We get to see the actors dressed up in old-fashioned costumes, or outlandish sci-fi garb, standing around sipping coffee and talking to the guy with a clipboard wearing jeans and a t-shirt. The cameramen are ready to roll. Production assistants run around putting the final props into place. Someone is worried about not having enough light to film the next scene, and someone else is shouting at everyone to take their places. Eventually, the director will shout "Action!" and the movie magic begins.

In a story, the "action" is called the *plot*. While plotlines can vary, most follow the pattern set out by Aristotle twenty-three centuries ago. Stories usually begin with *exposition* to provide some background information about the setting and characters. Then the *inciting incident* changes the status quo by introducing conflict. *Rising action* follows as the characters deal with the conflict, usually coming up against additional difficulties, before reaching the *climax* of the story. *Falling action* sees the characters dealing with the consequences of the climax, now that the hero is sure to win or lose, and the *denouement* (or *resolution*) ties up the loose ends and concludes the story.

The *inciting incident* of the plot can be a girl being told she can't go to a ball (Disney's *Cinderella*), a surgeon losing the use of his hands in a serious car accident (*Dr. Strange*), or a paratrooper dropping behind enemy lines in World War II the same day his three brothers are killed in action (*Saving Private Ryan*). Best-selling novelist Dean Koontz calls this pivotal part of the story "plunging the characters into terrible trouble." The rest of the story will be changed because of this incident, and the main character or characters will be changed as well.

In the table below, see if you can identify the inciting incident and the climax of a book you've read recently or a movie you've seen. Or you can choose a classic tale like *Cinderella*.

Name of Story:	
Inciting Incident:	
Climax:	

A PLOT SUMMARY

When I was in college, if you didn't want to read a whole book required for a class you would go to the college bookstore and buy a small book called *Cliff Notes* which would provide a summary of the plot and a literary analysis of the assigned book. Today, you can find plot summaries of books and movies on Wikipedia, IMDb, or other websites. They provide a general idea of a story and help you decide if you want to invest time reading the book or watching the movie. They can even help you understand a story better by seeing it from another person's perspective. But there are some things a plot summary will skip over or misinterpret, so it's best if you go to the original source and check it out for yourself.

Here is a short plot summary of Genesis, the first book of the Bible, from *The AMG Concise Bible Commentary*:

Adam and Eve, though sinless when created, fell into sin, and the evil consequences of their sin passed on to the human race descended from them. Rebellious humanity deserved, and received, God's judgment, but that judgment was always mixed with mercy. God did not destroy the human life he had created. Rather he worked through it to provide a way of salvation available to all. His way was to choose one man (Abraham), from whom he would build a nation (Israel), through which he would make his will known and eventually produce the Saviour of the world (Jesus).[39]

Here we have:

- *exposition*: Adam and Eve were created without sin;
- *an inciting incident*: they fell into sin;
- *rising action*: humanity suffers from the consequences of that sin, but God is at work through the characters in the story to provide a remedy to the trouble;
- and a foreshadow of *the climax* still to come when Jesus arrives to "crush" the "head" of Satan and bring redemption to Adam's race (Genesis 3:15).

This brief outline of Genesis actually sums up much of the Bible and is a good starting place to understand a Christian worldview. But what if Adam and Eve didn't really exist? What if the world developed over billions of years and humans descended from single-cell organisms? Is the suffering and evil in our world a result of sin and its consequences, or is there another explanation?

IN THE BEGINNING

Before we jump to the inciting incident, we need to have a better understanding of the exposition in God's story. There was a *way things were* before the *way things are now*.

Look up and write out the first five verses of Genesis 1:

_____

_____

_____

_____

_____

_____

_____

_____

_____

_____

_____

_____

_____

_____

Most Christians are familiar with these verses. They tell us that our story had a beginning and that God—who existed before the beginning—brought "the heavens and the earth" into being. The verses that follow say God made the land and the seas, the sun and the stars, the plants and the animals, and the first human beings. For non-Christians who don't believe in the Bible at all, this is pure make-believe. But even Christians have long debated whether this was written as a factual, historical accounting of the beginning of our world or if it's not meant to be read literally.

Today, some people may be surprised or even shocked to discover others still believe God created the world in six days. Scientists proclaim as fact that the earth is billions of years old and all life on the planet is the result of evolutionary processes. Many Christians see no conflict between believing the Bible and believing in science, while others claim the scientists are simply wrong and the only way to understand our world is to believe in a literal reading of Genesis 1. Many others say, "I believe God created the world, but it doesn't matter how He did it or how long it took."

In some ways, it doesn't matter, because there's nothing we can change about the beginning of our story. But understanding the beginning—and in particular, the inciting incident—helps us better understand what is going on in the middle of the story, the place we find ourselves, and that is very important! Before we can understand the inciting incident, we need some understanding of *the way things were* before the trouble started.

THOUGHTS ON "IN THE BEGINNING"

The exposition in Genesis 1-2 reveals a world made intentionally and methodically. It shows a world where everything has a purpose and a role to fulfill. And it tells us the nature of that world and the first humans who inhabited it: "God saw all that he had made, *and it was very good*" (Genesis 1:31, emphasis mine). As early as the fourth century, Christian scholars were debating whether these verses should be taken literally. Advances in science fueled that debate from the time of the Renaissance until Charles Darwin's pronouncement that it was natural processes, and not God, which brought about all the forms of life we find on our planet. Today, there are many views about the meaning of Genesis 1-2. Here are some general descriptions of the different views:

IT'S A MYTH

A group of biblical scholars in the late eighteenth and early nineteenth centuries concluded that the first books of the Bible were written by at least four different authors over a period of hundreds of years, long after the events listed in the books would have occurred. These different, and sometimes inconsistent, accounts of Israel's history were each written for a different purpose and were later compiled into the Old Testament as we know it today. This theory challenged not only the traditional view that Moses authored the first five books of the Bible but also that those books were divinely inspired and factually reliable. With such a view of the writing of Genesis 1-2, there is no reason to believe the creation story is anything other than a myth, possibly based on stories handed down for generations by ancestors of the Israelites.

IT'S AN ALLEGORY

The famed Christian theologian Augustine of Hippo (354-430 AD) taught that God created everything but not necessarily in the way described in Genesis. According to Augustine, God clearly made the world, but the account in Genesis 1 of a six-day creation is best understood as an allegory to help us understand our relationship to God and our need to return to God, be baptized, and bear the fruit of good works.[40] Augustine personally believed the universe was created all at once rather than in six days,[41] but he was open to other interpretations which took into account what could be learned from the world around us.[42]

Since Augustine's time, many other theologians have also interpreted the Genesis story as allegory rather than history. Some point to the poetic nature of the first chapter of Genesis to argue the passage is an illustration of how our universe was made in an orderly and purposeful manner, not that it was made in a certain way or a particular timeframe. Others believe the passage was intended to show the differences between the God of Israel (a loving creator, outside and superior to His creation) and the gods of other Middle Eastern ancient religions (vindictive beings, part of the created world and subject to it). These theologians see no need to refute the claim of scientists that the earth is billions of years old because they believe the Genesis story is not describing any historical events.

IT'S A CONDENSED VERSION OF HISTORY

Still other students of the Bible suggest the narrative in Genesis 1 is essentially true, but it's possible to read a long period of time into the account.

In the gap theory, it is suggested that "God created the heavens and the earth" as stated in Genesis 1:1, but He allowed the earth to develop for a long time—a time when dinosaurs roamed the earth, died, and were buried under many layers of dirt and rock. Then God decided to begin anew and flooded the earth leaving it "formless and empty" and covered in "the waters" found in Genesis 1:2. New life-forms, including the first humans, were then created over a six-day period.

A different idea, the day-age theory, suggests that each "day" mentioned in Genesis 1 refers to an "age" rather than a 24-hour period, and each age of creation could have taken millions or billions of years. God set the process of creation into motion (Genesis 1:1-2) and then intervened at certain points to create something new, such as the first plant life, the first animals, and the first humans (Genesis 1:3-31). A literal Adam and Eve could have been made at some point during this process, either 6,000 years ago or much earlier.

IT'S A LITERAL ACCOUNT OF A HISTORIC EVENT

Finally, there are Christians who believe in a literal reading of Genesis 1-2 and prefer to understand scientific discoveries in light of the Bible instead of understanding the Bible in light of ever-changing scientific discoveries. They argue that the fossil record and other geological evidence of the earth's old age can be explained by the worldwide flood described in Genesis 6-8. They also point out that scientific conclusions about the age of the universe and the origins of life are based on many assumptions, any one of which could be wrong.

Another way to explain the apparent age of the earth and the universe is to believe that God made everything in the Genesis 1 account in a mature condition. Adam was made as an adult man. Trees and bushes were full-grown and bearing fruit. Animals were already roaming. Birds were already flying (answering the old question, "Which came first, the chicken or the egg?").

The mountains could have already had layers, and the night sky could have already been filled with the glow of stars millions of lightyears away. The set was carefully prepared and frozen for one moment while the universe waited for the Director to yell, "Action!" Then Adam was made from the dust of the ground, and our story began.

WHY IT MATTERS

What a Christian believes about how our world began does matter because it affects the way he or she will understand many other things about the Bible. If we conclude that the narrative in the first two chapters of the Bible was entirely made up, it's easy to ignore any part of the Bible which isn't supported by current scientific or historical evidence (including the flood of Noah's day, the Hebrews being led from Egypt by Moses, or even the death and resurrection of Jesus). We are left with a highly unreliable tale that gives us little information about why we are here and what part we are to play in this ongoing story.

If we conclude the creation account is allegorical rather than literal, it leaves us with other questions. What did the world look like before sin entered the world? Did the world change somehow as a result of mankind's disobedience to God, or have death, decay, and brutality always been a part of the natural order?

How we answer these questions will affect our view of the rest of God's master story.

YOUR TURN

Earlier in this chapter, I asked you to write out the first five verses of Genesis 1. On the following page, you will find the last verse of that chapter. Read it over. Find some colored pencils and color in the words. Draw some pictures behind it, maybe of your favorite things about this world or the cosmos. While you are coloring, it would be a good time to discuss with your group how you think our world came into existence.

God saw all that
he had made, and
it was
very good.
And there was evening,
and there was morning
—the sixth day.
Genesis 1:31

7

INCITING INCIDENT

Most books and movies start with at least some exposition. We get a feel for the setting. We meet the main characters and maybe some of the minor ones. We see them going about normal life—maybe not normal for us, but normal for these characters in this setting. But before long, an event occurs which changes everything. This event which throws the story into a new direction is called the *inciting incident*. Something happens. Something bad, usually, or maybe something good. Something big, even if it's only important to one person in the story. The inciting incident shakes up the status quo, changes the equilibrium, and is "the primary cause for all that follows" in the rest of the story.[43]

For a story to matter to its audience, there must be some conflict that personally affects the main character or characters. Something happens which causes their world to change and creates in them a need or a desire to do something about it. The life of the protagonist has been thrown out of balance, and he needs to find a way to fix the problem, to gain what he needs, and to restore balance. According to Robert McKee, "the Inciting Incident propels the protagonist into an active pursuit of this object or goal . . . [It] pitches the protagonist's life out of kilter, arousing a conscious desire for something he feels will set things right, and he goes after it."[44]

See if you can match the following stories with their inciting incidents. (It's okay to look them up on IMDb or Wikipedia if you're not familiar with them.)*

---

* The answers can be found at the end of the chapter.

Jurassic World (2015)	A local bookstore owner learns that a large chain bookstore is being built across the street
Hamlet (circa 1600)	A video game villain is made to feel unwelcome at a party in honor of the game's anniversary
You've Got Mail (1998)	A large and deadly genetically engineered dinosaur escapes from an enclosure in a theme park
North by Northwest (1959)	An ordinary man is mistaken for a government agent
Wreck-It Ralph (2012)	The Prince of Denmark learns his mother will marry his uncle less than a month after his father's death

IDENTIFYING THE PROBLEM

Sometimes it can be difficult to figure out what event qualifies as the inciting incident in a story. The easiest way to identify it is to ask some questions: What is the major problem or change in the story the characters are dealing with? When did that problem or change start? When did the protagonist become aware of this disruption in his or her own status quo? Identifying the problem (trouble, conflict, shift in status quo) in a story and how it started is the key to understanding the rest of the story. McKee says: "The plot points that come after the inciting incident will always be related back to that point because it is the launching point that sets the character on a journey."[45]

In your own life, what do you think are the three biggest problems or challenges you are dealing with right now?

1.   _____

2.   _____

3. _____

In modern times, what do you think are the three biggest problems or challenges our world is dealing with?

1. _____

2. _____

3. _____

Looking at the whole history of the world, what is the one biggest challenge that humans have grappled with?

1. _____

The traditional Christian answer to this last question is SIN. According to the Westminster Shorter Catechism, "All mankind by their fall lost communion with God, are under his wrath and curse, and so made liable to all the miseries of this life, to death itself, and to the pains of hell forever."[46] Or, in the words of theologian Stanley J. Grenz:

> [H]umans show forth the workings of evil. Although created to respond to God and to others, we readily grow self-centered and apathetic, closing ourselves up within our own little universes. Designed to imitate the Creator through our creative abilities, we readily misuse the good gifts God has bestowed on us, destroy what others have constructed, and plunder the good world God made to nourish us. Above all, rather than reflecting God's own character, we display the malice of the evil one. In short, we whom God intends to be the crown of creation are fallen creatures. This dark side of the human situation is what the biblical authors term "sin." They forthrightly declare what human experience through the centuries confirms, namely, that something went wrong in the universe, and mankind stands at the center of the derailing of God's good intention.[47]

UNDERSTANDING THE PROBLEM

In God's master story, the big problem we're dealing with is sin. But what is sin, and when did it start? What was the inciting incident that changed our world from the *way things were* to the *way things are now*?

The Bible provides a simple answer to this question. Adam and Eve sinned in the Garden of Eden, and death and corruption entered the world through that sin (Romans 5:12-14; 1 Corinthians 15:21-22). Theologians have differed on exactly how that first sin infected the rest of humanity, but traditional Christian answers to "What went wrong?" all involve Adam and Eve.[48] Below are five different viewpoints expressed by theologians about the thorny question of sin:

OUR GUILT IS INHERITED FROM ADAM

One view is that Adam represented the whole of humanity before God. When he made a choice to disregard God's command, he doomed his entire family (the human race) to the effects of sin. Every human stands accused before God because of Adam's guilt, regardless of how good or bad we try to live our lives. A variation of this belief is that we were all literally present in Adam's body—a very part of his DNA that would be passed down to generations of humans—and so we all share in his guilt.

OUR SIN NATURE IS INHERITED FROM ADAM

Another view is that Adam and Eve physically passed a sin nature on to all their children. We are not born as a "blank slate" but with a propensity to be selfish, deceptive, and prideful and to reject God's rule over our hearts and lives. We sin because of Adam, but we are found guilty on the basis of our own actions and not those of our forefather.

OUR DEPRAVITY IS INHERITED FROM ADAM

A similar view is that we inherited a fallen or depraved[49] nature from Adam. Rather than being blamed for Adam's sin, we are born into a state of being which is less than the perfect holiness of God. We "fall short of the glory of God," as Paul says (Romans 3:23), and because of that, "there is no one who understands; there is no one who seeks God. All have turned away, they have together become worthless; there is no one who does good, not even one" (Romans 3:11-12). It is this depraved state, rather than any specific sin, that separates us from God.

Of course, all of these answers to "What is the big problem?" assume that Adam and Eve were real, historical people as described in the first chapters of the Bible. The first humans were placed in a world without sin or corruption. Their disobedience brought sin and its consequences into their lives and the lives of all their descendants. Christians who believe in a literal six-day creation also point to Adam's sin as the cause of death and decay in the physical world. God told Adam, "Cursed is the ground because of you; . . . It will produce thorns and thistles for you" (Genesis 3:17-18). The very first death occurred when God sacrificed an animal to make garments of skin to cover Adam and Eve's nakedness. The inciting incident in this Christian worldview was Adam's sin, which produced a dramatic change in the status quo of both humans and the world we live in.

Other Christians who believe in a literal Adam and Eve, but who prefer to read a long time period into the creation story of Genesis 1-3, also point to Adam's first sin as the cause of our broken relationship with God and the lingering effects of sin in the lives of all humans. However, they accept the idea that the world had already existed for millions or billions of years before Adam's fall. If animal and plant life evolved and covered the earth long before Adam lived, then physical decay and death preceded Adam's sin and were part of the natural order of the world as God originally designed it. In this worldview, the inciting incident of Adam's sin produced a radical change for humans but had less of an effect on our environment. Our sinful actions can harm the world we live in, but death and decay, deadly animals, illnesses, natural disasters, and climate change would be part of the story even without the fall of mankind.

Finding the cause of our problems becomes more difficult for Christians who believe the first chapters of Genesis should be read allegorically instead of historically. For these Christians, Adam was not a real person, but a symbol of humankind (as a race or as individuals). In this view, it doesn't matter if the human race started with two uniquely created individuals or whole tribes of evolved mammals finally able to comprehend the existence of God and the nature of good and evil. What matters is that at some point, in some way, something went wrong in the relationship between God and man.

ADAM SYMBOLIZES THE SINS WHICH MAKE MANKIND GUILTY BEFORE GOD

In one variation of this worldview, the story of Adam and Eve represents the ongoing story of humans who, one after another, succumb to an external temptation and fall into a state of sin. Like the allegorical Adam and Eve, we have each been offered choices in our life between good and evil, and when we choose evil, even once, our own sin makes us guilty before God. However, there are two problems with this view when it is argued out to a logical conclusion. If we are all born innocent, we either have the ability to remain innocent (never sin) or we do not have this ability and are inherently predisposed to sin. The first possibility, that humans are capable of never sinning, goes against the teaching of the Bible and was condemned as heresy at the Council of Ephesus in 431 AD.[50] The second possibility is that humans have been naturally predisposed to sin since the beginning (since no literal Adam and Eve got the ball started). This suggests that either God made us inherently sinful and rebellious or we evolved this way over time—both of which raise many questions about the goodness of God and His original creation.

ADAM SYMBOLIZES THE CORRUPTION OF CREATION WHICH SEPARATES US FROM GOD

Another way to look at the story of Adam and Eve allegorically is to assume that at some point sin entered the world through our human ancestors and forever changed the relationship between man and God, man and our environment, and among all humans. We all suffer from the earliest sin, whatever and whenever it was, because we are all born into a fallen world. Personal sin becomes less relevant in this worldview, and it is possible to conclude that humans are capable of avoiding individual sin, even if they cannot avoid living in a world contaminated by the sins of our ancestors and neighbors. Similar to the last viewpoint, this one also disagrees with the teachings of the Bible and the Church.

WHY IT MATTERS

The main portion of any story is the work of the protagonist to achieve a particular goal. This goal is a direct response to the inciting incident near the beginning of the story. It may be to restore the status quo which existed before the inciting incident, or it may be to move on to a better life than the character had before. If the characters in the story don't fully understand the problem they're dealing with, they will have a difficult time fixing it or getting past it. According to writing instructor James Hull: "Every problem has a solution, and a story explores that process of trying to attain resolution."[51]

For some people being a Christian means nothing more than accepting a set of propositions about God and Jesus and following the rules found in the Bible or taught by a particular church. But, as I argued in Chapter Two, it takes much more than that to really know God and to take an active part in the work He is doing in the world. Understanding God's work in the world starts with understanding the problem which needs to be resolved. It is a critical part of our worldview—far too critical for us to sit back and say it doesn't matter how the world started or where humans came from or what happened between our earliest ancestors and God. It matters tremendously because, in one way or another, it affects *our* relationship with God.

The Catholic Catechism summarizes the discussion well:

> Among all the Scriptural texts about creation, the first three chapters of Genesis occupy a unique place ... The inspired authors have placed them at the beginning of Scripture to express in their

solemn language the truths of creation- its origin and its end in God, its order and goodness, the vocation of man, and finally the drama of sin and the hope of salvation . . . [T]hese texts remain the principal source for [understanding] the mysteries of the 'beginning': creation, fall, and promise of salvation.[52]

For Christians of every denomination, the first three chapters of Genesis are the principal source for understanding the rest of God's master story. Before dismissing them as myth or legend, or even allegory, we should seriously consider what God meant to reveal through them regarding himself, the world He created, and our place in it.

YOUR TURN

Go back to Chapter 3 and look at your response to the statement "I believe the Bible is God's Word and is true." On a scale of zero to 100%, how much did you agree with that statement then? _____ Would you change that percentage now? If so, to what? _____

In Chapter 3 we discussed different beliefs about the authorship of the Bible. In light of what we've been learning, I would like you to now mark the position you believe is correct:

[ ] The Bible was written by humans without any intervention from God

[ ] The Bible was written by God through humans who transcribed His very words

[ ] The Bible was written by God through humans who wrote from their own perspective but were inspired by God

Use the following lines to journal your thoughts about how the authorship and reliability of the Bible affect your personal belief in the events recorded in the first three chapters of the Bible:

_____

_____

THE CHAPTER CHALLENGE

Near the beginning of the chapter, could you match the story with a description of its inciting incident? The inciting incidents in the order they're listed are from *You've Got Mail, Wreck-It Ralph, Jurassic World, North by Northwest,* and *Hamlet.*

8

GOALS

Now we're getting into the heart of the story. We have a setting. We have characters. We've seen something of the background of those characters, what was once normal for them, then we watched as the inciting incident upset the status quo and changed the course of the story. Next, the characters react. They figure out as best they can what went wrong, and they start out on a course of action intending to make things right.

McKee describes this important element as follows:

> "[T]he Inciting Incident first throws the protagonist's life out of balance, then arouses in him the desire to restore that balance. Out of this need, . . . the protagonist next conceives of an Object of Desire: something . . . he feels he lacks or needs to put the ship of life on an even keel. Lastly, the Inciting Incident propels the protagonist into an active pursuit of this object or goal."[53]

What I said in the last chapter bears repeating: The main portion of any story is the work of the protagonist to achieve a particular *goal*. The goal may be to restore the status quo which existed before the inciting incident, or it may be to move on to a better life than the character had before. If the characters in the story don't fully understand the problem they're dealing with, they will have a difficult time fixing it or getting past it. As Hull explains: "Every problem has a solution, and a story explores that process of trying to attain resolution."[54]

Below are some common goals used in stories. Next to each goal, write the name of one book, movie, or play in which this is the major goal of the story.

To stop a villain:_____

_____

To get the girl (or guy):_____

_____

To return home:_____

_____

To survive:_____

_____

To prove one's worth:_____

_____

DIFFERENT CHARACTERS, DIFFERENT GOALS

As we have learned, every story needs a protagonist—one or more characters moving toward a goal. The protagonist has a conscious desire and the will to create change. They have been affected by the inciting incident and want things to be different than they have become. When a story has more than one protagonist, they may be working toward the same goal, together or separately, or they may be working toward different goals, each with their own idea of what it will take to resolve the conflict created by the inciting incident.

At the beginning of God's master story, we are introduced to two main characters: God (the Creator of heaven and earth) and mankind (Adam and Eve literally or as a representation of humanity). Later, we'll come back to other characters introduced in the first chapters of Genesis, but let's focus on these two characters first.

GOD'S ROLE

There are three ways to look at God's role in the story. Some people believe God was involved in making our world but He has been pretty much "hands-off" ever since, leaving His created beings to figure out for themselves how to live in this world and find some sense of purpose in it. There are variations on this belief, from God being completely absent from the continuing story (which is a Deist worldview, and not a Christian one), to God providing some guidance by occasionally interacting with His created beings. People who dismiss the truth of the Bible by claiming it was not inspired by God may still find some historical evidence of God's work in the world, but it's very difficult for them to make a strong argument for what they believe to be the purpose or plan behind His involvement.

Others look at God as a primary protagonist in the story. He created the heavens and earth, put mankind on the earth to rule it for Him, and declared everything "very good" (Genesis 1:31). But mankind's disobedience radically changed the status quo of God's design. Sin and evil were not part of the original plan, and God's goal ever since then has been to remedy the problem of sin and evil in some way. This, of course, raises the question of why God created us the way He did, capable of sinning and ruining His good creation, if He never intended for us to do so. But we'll get to that question later.

Finally, some Christians believe the fall of mankind was always part of God's plan, just as the inciting incident is an intentional part of any author's story. Sin changed the way God relates to mankind, but it didn't take Him by surprise or change His long-term goals. I love the way J.R.R. Tolkien expressed this view in *The Silmarillion*. In this epic prequel to *The Hobbit* and *The Lord of the Rings,* Tolkien tells the story of the creation of Middle Earth, the fall of the Elves, and what happened afterward. Responding to the fall, an angelic being predicts that "beauty not before conceived [shall] be brought forth . . . and evil yet be good to have been."

"And yet remain evil," his colleague replies.[55]

While the first two chapters of Genesis give us some idea of how God created the heavens and the earth, they don't say a lot about *why* He created them. When God stepped back at the end of Day 6 and proclaimed His creation "very good" (Genesis 1:31), what did He intend to happen on days 7, 8, and 9? Genesis 1:27-28 provides a clue to the answer, but, as usual, Christians disagree on how to interpret these verses:

> So God created mankind in his own image, in the image of God he created them; male and female he created them. God blessed them and said to them, "Be fruitful and increase in number; fill the earth and subdue it. Rule over the fish in the sea and the birds in the sky and over every living creature that moves on the ground."

Some Christians view these verses as evidence of God's long term plan for His creation—his "Creation Mandate."[56] He made mankind to rule as His stewards over the rest of the created realm—the earth, plants, animals, and, perhaps, eventually, the whole cosmos. Although God's original design was disrupted by mankind's sin and its consequences, God's ultimate plan remains the same—for mankind to rule the earth.

However, Christians vary widely in how they believe God intends to achieve this goal. Some believe He will simply start over—destroying this creation and replacing it with "a new heaven and a new earth" (Revelation 21:1-5). Others believe God, at some future time, will renew this creation in the same way He will provide new resurrection bodies to believers. Creation will be different, better, but not entirely new (see Romans 8:19-21). Still others believe God is already at work transforming this creation through the work of His people within their cultures.

What these views have in common is seeing God's ultimate goal as a do-over of His original plan. Whether creation is replaced, renewed, or slowly restored, the focus of God's plan is to return to His original design of mankind ruling with Him over a good creation.

Other Christians disagree that Genesis 1:28 sets forth a "Creation Mandate" revealing God's full plan for mankind. In this view, humans were not commanded but rather designed to be fruitful, a word that can refer to physical reproduction as well as using the earth's resources to devise and develop new things. In the same way, humans were designed to "rule over the fish in the sea and the birds in the sky and over every living creature that moves on the ground" (Genesis 1:28). It is simply part of their nature, just as it is in the nature of fish to fill the seas and birds to fill the skies (Genesis 1:20-22).

With this interpretation of mankind's beginning, we are left without a definitive answer to what God's eventual plan is for His creation. Filling and subduing the earth could be seen as a temporary pastime while God prepared mankind for other tasks. Sin entered the world, either as part of God's plan or as a detour, but God is still at work to prepare the pinnacle of His creation—mankind—for the eternal work (or rest) He has in store. In other words, God's goal isn't to go back to the original plan envisioned in the Garden of the Eden. Instead, the plan has always been to move forward to something better—something we can now only guess at and anticipate.

Whatever we think God's goal is, perhaps the most important thing we need to ask is this: Do we truly believe God has the ability to reach His goal and bring about the end of the story He desires? Can He really bring about the good He intends to resolve all that has gone wrong in the story? If we don't really believe in God's power and ability to reach His ultimate goal, this is all just an interesting theological debate that will have no impact on our daily lives.

As I quoted in Chapter 1, a person's worldview "provides the very foundation on which we live and move and have our being."[57] The most important point of any worldview is what we believe about God and what He is doing in the world. No matter what we believe about God's plan and purpose, if we don't believe He has the power to do it—that He WILL do it—we don't have a very firm foundation on which to stand.

The second character we meet at the beginning of God's story is mankind: "So God created mankind in his own image, in the image of God he created them; male and female he created them" (Genesis 1:27). While mankind was clearly affected by the inciting incident of sin entering the world, humanity would be a protagonist in the story only if we have the desire and the ability to change the direction of the story. Both history and personal experience testify to mankind's desire to change his circumstances, but do we have the ability to do so?

Theologians have long debated the relationship between humanity's free will and God's sovereignty (His right and ability to do whatever He chooses). Do humans have the ability to choose their own course of action, or does God direct everything that happens? Do we choose freely to accept or reject salvation, or has that decision been predetermined by God? Or are we humans little more than puppets on a stage with God pulling all the strings? Or is there a middle ground?

On the extremes of the beliefs, some proclaim God is fully sovereign and nothing can occur apart from His will, while others say God has willingly limited His sovereignty, or is limited in nature, so mankind can freely act in opposition to God's will. Most Christians fall somewhere in the middle of this debate. Even those who believe in the doctrine of *election** usually also believe humans have freedom of choice. While ultimate *self-determination*** is something only God can claim, most Christians believe humans do have the ability and freedom to make choices, and we are responsible for those choices.

While it can be difficult to reconcile the concepts of man's free will and God's sovereignty, many have tried to do so. Others simply accept both

---

*   The doctrine of election is the belief that God has chosen in advance all the people who will be saved or redeemed. Only the elect are capable of becoming Christians.

**   Ultimate self-determination refers to a state of being in which no other person or power can control the choices an individual makes.

as biblical truths even though they appear contradictory or paradoxical. Christian author Kenneth Boa writes:

> Mysteries are forced upon us by the facts of God's Word; we are not inventing them ourselves. Since His written revelation teaches concepts that appear to be mutually exclusive, we must realize that with God both truths are friends, not enemies. In God's higher rationality, things that we think must be either-or can in reality be both-and.[58]

MAN'S GOALS

If we assume humans possess some degree of free will, we can consider mankind to be a protagonist in the story and look at the goals we are pursuing. As stated above, the goal of a protagonist is directly related to that character's understanding of the inciting incident. What do they think went wrong? What do they believe is broken or out of balance? What goal or goals are they pursuing to try and resolve the conflict of the story?

The Old Testament is largely a narrative of people pursuing one goal after another to try to reach some Object of Desire they thought would resolve their problems. What did they desire?

- To be like God (Genesis 3:5)
- To be accepted by God on their own terms instead of God's (Genesis 4:1-8)
- To make a name for themselves (Genesis 11:4)
- To pursue physical pleasures without boundaries (Judges 19:20-26)
- To add to their own riches at the expense of others (Psalm 10:2-3; Proverbs 1:10-14)
- To escape death (Psalm 89:47-48)

Over time and throughout the world, men and women have continued to pursue these goals and many others. Humans have a deep sense of something missing, and they look for many different ways to fill the void: fame, financial security, family, accomplishments, adrenaline, sex, food, or power. Others succumb to the feeling that they will never feel complete. Instead of trying to fill the void in their lives, they simply try to mask it and dull the pain they feel deep inside.

Oftentimes, a protagonist in a story will have multiple goals, even conflicting ones. A character's conscious goal—what he thinks he wants—may be completely different from his unconscious goal—what he actually wants or needs. Is this not the perfect description of humanity? Apart from God, we seek to find a resolution to our needs in everything that is *not* God when all the time our souls long to be mended by the only One who can satisfy our wants and meet our needs, the very One we are trying so hard to live without.

Unfortunately, turning to God and becoming a Christian does not completely remove this conflict in our lives. What it can do—and should do—is change the dynamic. Both consciously and subconsciously we will continue to battle the desire to have our own way, but our primary goal should now be to surrender our personal goals and substitute them with God's. Our view of God's goal for our individual lives will differ based on our understanding of God's overall goal for His creation, but there are some biblical directives most would agree should guide our lives:

> "He has shown you, O mortal, what is good. And what does the Lord require of you? To act justly and to love mercy and to walk humbly with your God" (Micah 6:8).

> Jesus replied: "'Love the Lord your God with all your heart and with all your soul and with all your mind.' This is the first and greatest commandment. And the second is like it: 'Love your neighbor as yourself.' All the Law and the Prophets hang on these two commandments" (Matthew 22:37-40).

> Then Jesus came to them and said, "All authority in heaven and on earth has been given to me. Therefore go and make disciples of

all nations, baptizing them in the name of the Father and of the Son and of the Holy Spirit, and teaching them to obey everything I have commanded you. And surely I am with you always, to the very end of the age" (Matthew 28:18-20).

YOUR TURN

Throughout the Bible, we see that God is not just interested in the big picture. He cares about each of us—how we live and the choices we make. It's amazing to think that His plan for the whole of creation includes a plan for each person He calls His own.

In Chapter 7, I asked you to write out the three biggest problems or challenges you are dealing with in your own life right now. Choose one of those problems and describe how you might respond if your goal was to achieve your own personal needs. Then write out how you would respond if your goal was to help God achieve His goals for your life.

The Problem: _____

_____

_____

_____

_____

_____

_____

_____

_____

Pursuing my own goal: _____

_____

_____

_____

_____

_____

_____

_____

_____

_____

Pursuing God's goal: _____

_____

_____

_____

_____

_____

_____

_____

_____

_____

_____

9

OBSTACLES AND OPPOSITION

The goals of the characters may be obvious immediately after the inciting incident, or they may become clear only as time passes. What is important is that we see the characters in action. The protagonist of the story will not sit by passively waiting for something to happen. He acts. He pursues the goal he believes will set everything right again. As he pursues his goal, he is certain to come up against obstacles and opposition. Someone or something is standing in the way of his heart's desire. In most stories, there will be a progression of obstacles, each one more difficult than the last to overcome.

According to McKee: "When the protagonist steps out of the Inciting Incident, he enters a world governed by the Law of Conflict. To wit: *Nothing moves forward in a story except through conflict.*"⁵⁹

While we accept and even expect conflict and complications in fictional stories, most of us would be happy to live without them in our real lives. But conflict, obstacles, and opposition are part of all our lives. McKee goes on to explain:

> Story is metaphor for life, and to be alive is to be in seemingly perpetual conflict. As Jean-Paul Sartre expressed it, the essence of reality is scarcity, a universal and eternal lacking. There isn't enough of anything to go around. Not enough food, not enough love, not enough justice, and never enough time. Time, as Heidegger observed is the basic category of existence. We live in its ever-shrinking shadow, and if we are to achieve anything in

our brief being that lets us die without feeling we've wasted our time, we will have to go into heady conflict with the forces of scarcity that deny our desires.[60]

But why is life on Earth so complicated? Why do we have to fight so hard for what we desire? If there is a God who created the heavens and the earth, why did He make things this way? Why did He make *us* this way?

THE BIG QUESTIONS

No one gets very far in life before they start asking "why?" questions.

- Why is this happening to me?
- Why can't I have what I want?
- Why is everything so difficult?
- Why can't I just be happy?

When we reach the stage of asking the biggest question—"Why did God allow this?"—many people turn away and choose to not believe in God. Others push the questions away and choose to believe in God without really thinking about what that means or how it should affect their lives. Still other Christians have grappled with the big questions and tried to come up with reasonable answers. Let's look at some of those big questions now.

BIG QUESTION 1: WHY DOES GOD ALLOW EVIL IN THE WORLD?

As we discussed in the last chapter, there are three general views of God's role in the master story. Those views affect the way people answer this question.

(1) If God is mostly absent from the ongoing story, one might conclude He doesn't care about what we view as evil in the world. He may have set creation into motion and then watched as plants and animals evolved, the strong overcame the weak, and death and decay kept the profusion of life in check. In this view, humans are not so much evil as they are biologically programmed to survive in a harsh environment of scarce resources. This is very similar to the argument of the atheist who says there is no absolute moral law, only evolutionary instinct which has worked its way into institutional

customs. (Or, as Voldemort told Harry Potter, "There is no good and evil—only power, and those too weak to seek it."[61])

(2) If God is a primary protagonist in the story, trying to fix what went wrong in His good creation, there are two ways to approach the question. First, you might doubt God's *omniscience* (that He is all-knowing) or His *omnipotence* (that He is all-powerful). Perhaps God didn't know what would happen when He placed humans on the earth, so the fall of mankind and the resulting evil in the world all came as a surprise. Or perhaps He was unable to create a world where evil could not enter. However, neither of these ideas is supported by the Bible.

A more common answer is that God intentionally created humans with free will fully aware that they might (or even would) choose to disobey Him. Why? Because freedom was an important part of His plan. His creation would not have been "very good" (Genesis 1:31) if it contained only beings with no ability to appreciate Him and *choose* to love Him. If God's goals in creating us included a desire to share His love or to reveal His glory, it was necessary to create beings who could freely receive that love or willingly reflect that glory.

We would not be made "in the image of God" if we didn't have the ability to make meaningful choices, including the choice to reject God's plan for our lives (Genesis 1:27). Ravi Zacharias and Vince Vitale explore this idea in their book, *Why Suffering?: Finding Meaning and Comfort When Life Doesn't Make Sense.* They conclude: "Love and forgiveness, worth and worship—all are conditional on freedom."[62] And true freedom comes with consequences. The free will God created within us allows us to choose evil over good and ourselves over God. The pain and suffering we see in our fallen world are a result of our free choices, not God's.

(3) Finally, we have the possibility that God always intended that sin and evil would be a part of His creation. The "why" gets bigger and louder here. One possible answer is that "God, who knows all things, allows evils whose

absence would diminish even greater goods."[63] As humans, we could not fully appreciate the glory of God if we never experienced anything opposed to that glory, just as we could not appreciate a cold drink if we had never been thirsty or a warm fire if we had never been cold. The greatest love God could show for us was to join us in our suffering, and we would never have known that love without sin and suffering in our world.

Sin and evil also have a refining purpose in the lives of Christians. When we choose to pursue God's goals instead of our own, the result of our new pursuit is a special kind of "fruit": "love, joy, peace, patience, kindness, goodness, faithfulness, gentleness, self-control" (Galatians 5:22-23, ESV). You don't wake up one day and have patience or self-control. You acquire these characteristics with lots of practice dealing with situations you can't control. It's not hard to be kind, good, or gentle when you have everything you need, but nothing is more moving than watching a person who has suffered hardship and loss offer a helping hand or a kind word to someone else. And what are love and faithfulness when they have never been tested by an opportunity to turn away and pursue an easier goal? Might not these worthy goals be a reason why God would intentionally put us in a world where sin and evil would reign until their work was done?

BIG QUESTION 2: WHAT ABOUT SATAN? WHAT'S HIS ROLE?

One other explanation for evil in our world is that it is the work of Satan, and not God's doing at all. Of course, Christians have different ways of understanding who or what Satan is and what his role is in the story. One view is that he does not exist. When writers of the books of the Bible mentioned Satan or the devil, they may have been talking about evil in a metaphorical way or they may have been writing from their own limited perspectives, attributing to supernatural forces things they couldn't understand such as mental illnesses and strong human desires.

A second view is that there *is* a supernatural being the Bible calls Satan (Mark 4:15), the devil (1 Peter 5:8), "the prince of this world" (John 12:31), "the god of this age" (2 Corinthians 4:4), and "the ruler of the kingdom of the air" (Ephesians 2:2). He might be described as the archenemy of God, the ultimate antagonist. His three main goals are to deceive us, to accuse us, and to tempt us to sin.

Some Christians think of Satan as being equal in power and authority to God. They see a cosmic struggle between good and evil being played out throughout history, similar to the "dark side" and "light side" of the "force" portrayed in *Star Wars* movies. Such a belief makes it easier to excuse God's failure to end sin and suffering and shifts the blame for continuing evil onto God's nemesis, but it also greatly weakens the doctrine of God's ultimate power and sovereignty. A religious worldview called Manichaeism, which taught that good and evil are equally powerful, was condemned in 382 AD as being opposed to Christian doctrine, but it continues to affect Christians today, often on a subconscious level.

A very different view is that Satan (as a being or as a force) has no power or authority of his own but acts only as an agent of God. In the Old Testament, the word Satan can be translated "an adversary, obstacle or stumbling block."[64] The Jews teach that these obstacles and stumbling blocks are placed in our way by God's design for our benefit.[65]

The predominant Christian view, however, is that Satan is one of God's creations, a powerful angel who rebelled against God and was cast out of heaven. Satan and the rest of the fallen angels (or demons) oppose God's plans and attempt to keep humans from being reconciled to God. However, they are inferior to God in every way and will one day be punished for their rebellion.

BIG QUESTION 3: IF GOD HAS A PLAN TO FIX THE PROBLEM OF SIN, WHAT IS STANDING IN THE WAY?

Whether or not sin and its consequences were an intended part of God's original design, the Bible proclaims that God has a plan to work everything out for good in the end (Romans 8:28). Christians don't all agree on the specifics of the goal or the plan to get us there, but we hope for an eternal future free from the sin, evil, pain, and suffering which mark our present existence. So, why doesn't God fix it now? What is standing in His way? Here are some possible answers to that question.

(1) *Satan and demons.* We've already talked about Satan, but it's important to note that while Satan may or may not be responsible for the beginning of evil, he may be a major reason why sin and evil continue today. Satan and his followers, called demons or impure spirits, are identified in the New Testament as working in opposition to all that is good: Jesus' mission (Matthew 4:1-11), physical and mental health (Matthew 9:32-33, 12:22; Mark 5:2-15); truth (2 Thessalonians 2:9-10; Acts 5:3); and the work of Christians (Ephesians 6:11-12). Satan was active in the Old Testament as well, working against the people of God (Genesis 3; 1 Chronicles 21:1, Job 1-2; and Zechariah 3:1-2). If these Biblical stories are true, it is at least possible these beings are still active in the world today.

(2) *Enemies of the Church.* In addition to spiritual opposition, there is plenty of human hostility toward God and His people. While this has been true throughout history, it's easiest to see the opposition we face today. In many countries around the world, it's dangerous or even illegal to be a Christian or to preach the Christian message. One Christian group estimates "approximately 215 million Christians now experience high, very high, or extreme levels of persecution; that means one in twelve Christians live where Christianity is 'illegal, forbidden, or punished.'"[66] In many other countries where they don't face physical harm, Christians are still ridiculed and scorned by people who hold opposing views. It's hard for us to pursue God's goals for our world when so many people are pursuing opposing goals.

Some Christians view all non-Christians as enemies of God's truth. Others see only those actively engaged in suppressing Christianity as their enemies. It's important to remember, though, the words of Christ to "love your enemies and pray for those who persecute you" (Matthew 5:43-48). After all, a person who is your enemy today could be your brother or sister in Christ tomorrow.

(3) *People of the Church.* If God's ultimate plan involves a restoration of the original created order through the work of His people, we might point the finger at God's own people for failing to aid in that restoration. If the "Creation Mandate" requires Christians to change their cultures, as some teach, then Christians who are not working toward that goal are delaying the fulfillment of God's plan. Other Christians believe God's mandate involves saving souls rather than reforming culture, but Christians still may be at fault in two ways. One, we aren't out there doing the job and, two, the way we live makes it harder for people to believe in God. Sometimes the greatest obstacle to people believing in the Christian message is the people delivering that message. It is said that Mahatma Gandhi studied the Bible and often quoted the teachings of Jesus, but he rejected Christianity because of the many Christians he knew who were so unlike Jesus in their actions.[67]

Why are we failing in our mission?

- Not everyone who calls themselves a Christian is a Christian. It's simply the default setting; if I'm not Jewish, Muslim, or some other religion, and I'm not an atheist, I must be a Christian.
- Other people have been introduced to Christianity and have accepted its basic beliefs, but they have never tried to live according to its teachings.
- Others hide behind the laws of God and use them as an excuse to hate and bully others who don't follow those laws—usually forgetting the second most important law in the Bible: "Love your neighbor as yourself" (Mark 12:28-31).
- Even the sincerest Christians make mistakes and fail in relationships, and even our best attempts at explaining our beliefs can be viewed as intolerance.

All this can be taken as evidence that the powerful, life-changing God we say we believe in doesn't exist.

(4) *Timing.* Whether any or all of the above reasons are true, it's also possible that God has not wrapped up His plan yet because He isn't ready to. The timing is not right. The work He is doing in and through His people has not yet been finished. The Bible tells us, "The Lord is not slow in keeping his promise, as some understand slowness. Instead he is patient with you, not wanting anyone to perish, but everyone to come to repentance" (2 Peter 3:9).

YOUR TURN

We covered a lot of material in this chapter without taking any breaks. Congratulations on making it through! Your reward is another Bible verse for coloring on the next page. But before you turn there, I have one challenge for you. Try to think of three different stories (movies, books, or even TV shows) in which the main character gained something good in the end, not *in spite* of the hardships he or she faced in pursuing their goal, but *because* of the obstacles and oppositions.

1._____

2._____

3._____

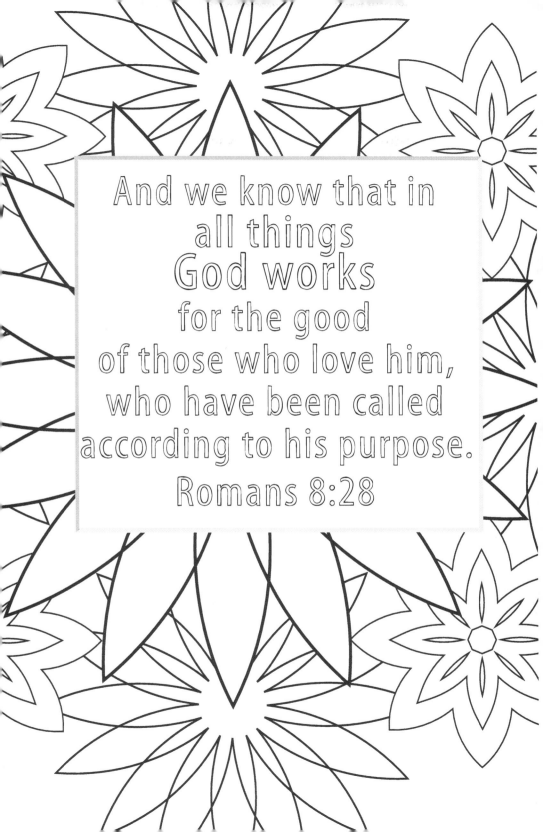

And we know that in
all things
God works
for the good
of those who love him,
who have been called
according to his purpose.
Romans 8:28

10

ULTIMATE CLIMAX

Conflict, unfulfilled desires, obstacles, opposition—where does it all end? Again and again, the protagonist attempts to reach his goal and set everything right. Again and again, he's thwarted. Ethan Hunt tries to stop a villain from obtaining a nuclear weapon only to see the weapon snatched away and placed where it can do the most damage to the greatest number of people (*Mission Impossible: Fallout*). Three astronauts hurtle through space in a damaged capsule short on power, short on air, and short on options (*Apollo 13*). Trapped in a job he hates, in a town he wants to escape, George Bailey's bad luck only gets worse when a large sum of money goes missing from his company (*It's a Wonderful Life*).

Eventually, the battle between the protagonist and the opposition reaches a peak. A decision will be made and action will be taken which will ensure a victory or leave the protagonist's goal forever out of reach. This height of conflict and tension in the story is called the *climax*: "the decisive moment in the story that all the action builds up to."[68]

The climax of a story does more than resolve the conflict. It also shows us the deepest truths about the protagonist's character and reveals what is most valued in the story itself. *Apollo 13* shows us that success can sometimes come from failure. In *It's a Wonderful Life*, we discover George Bailey's deepest desire isn't fame, adventure, or money, but the love of his family. The *Mission Impossible* movies tell us the "good guys" will always win over the "bad guys" (which can be true in a movie franchise but not always in real life). While not all stories end happily, they all have something to teach us when we, along with the main characters in the story, reach that moment of a last decision, a last action, and a desperate hope that all will work out well.

Think of your own favorite book or movie and write a description of the climax here: _____

_____

_____

_____

_____

_____

What did you learn about the main character at this crucial part of the story?

_____

_____

_____

_____

_____

DRAMATIC STRUCTURE

Writers of books and films don't all agree about the best way to build a story and what to call each part of the structure. Acts, scenes, turning points, crisis, and climax cannot always be neatly defined within a story. In general, though, stories have a rhythm of rising and falling action. The protagonist gets close to solving his problem only to be delayed by an obstacle in his path. He gets past the obstacle and moves forward again only to be thwarted by some new complication. Things get better. Things get worse. After many bumps in the road, we finally get to see the hero win the girl's heart, catch the bad guy, or stop the meteor from hitting the earth. A short resolution follows where we see the happy results of the hero's victory (or the sad aftermath of his defeat) and all the subplots of the story are wrapped up.

In the narrative found in the Bible, we also find a number of highs and lows as God and mankind work toward opposing goals. Mankind is created and placed in a bountiful world (high). Mankind sins and is placed under a curse (low). Mankind begins to fill the earth, cultivating the land and building cities (high). But people continue to sin against God, so He sends a flood to wipe out most of the life on earth (low). From the newly populated earth, God chooses one man to become the father of a nation God will use to bless the world (high). But that nation continually sins against God, so He sends them into captivity (low). Mankind proves it is unable to follow God's laws and "earn" God's blessings (really low), so God takes on flesh and enters the world to provide a means of salvation (high).

THE ROLE OF THE CROSS

Some writers use the term *climax* to refer to more than one event in a story. Each act can have a climax—a high point of action and danger—but it is not until the final act and the ultimate climax that the conflict is finally resolved one way or the other. In God's master story, the highest point of action reached so far would have to be Jesus' death on the cross and His resurrection from the dead. Belief in this historical event defines Christianity more than any other doctrine. Unfortunately, we don't all agree on what we should believe about the role and reach of the cross.

Here are some of the terms used in the Bible to describe the work of Jesus at the cross:

Atonement: This term focuses on the sin of mankind—both the sin of Adam affecting the whole race and the sins of each individual. Atonement means to make amends for something we did wrong—to fix the problem, repay the loss, or restore what was broken. The Bible says that humans are not capable of fixing our own sinfulness or paying off our debt to God. The just punishment for sin is death and eternal separation from the holy God (Romans 6:23; Revelation 20:12-13). Since humans cannot beat death, we "are destined to die once, and after that to face judgment" (Hebrews 9:27).

Only God is great enough to atone for our sins and make things right between us again. However, God is holy and just and cannot simply ignore our sin, so the cost of our sins still needs to be paid. Jesus paid that cost by taking our sins on Himself and dying a death He, being sinless, did not deserve. As 1 John 2:2 says: "He is the atoning sacrifice for our sins, and not only for ours but also for the sins of the whole world."

Redemption: This term also focuses on human sin, but it suggests that our sin left us in bondage to Satan and to sin itself. Although we are capable of doing good, we repeatedly make bad choices and do things that are wrong in God's eyes. As the slaves of sin and Satan, we needed someone to redeem us out of bondage and set us free to serve God. Hebrews 2:14-15 says that "since the children have flesh and blood, he too shared in their humanity so that by his death he might break the power of him who holds the power of death—that is, the devil—and free those who all their lives were held in slavery by their fear of death." And in Mark 10:45, Mark writes "for even the Son of man [Jesus] did not come to be served, but to serve, and to give his life as a ransom for many."

Justification: A third term involves the legal effect of Jesus' death for our sakes. When God declares us "justified" He is recognizing a change in our official status. We owed a debt to God, and that debt was paid on our behalf. We are no longer debtors. We are no longer condemned by the law. In fact, the last words of Jesus on the cross, "It is finished" (John 19:30), is a phrase commonly used in New Testament times on bills and business papers to indicate a debt was paid in full.[69] Romans 5:1 expresses this sentiment well:

"Therefore, since we have been justified through faith, we have peace with God through our Lord Jesus Christ."

Reconciliation: Another term focuses on a different effect of sin, the breaking of mankind's relationship with God. Theologian Donald G. Bloesch writes:

> The deepest meaning of the cross is that God, out of his incomparable love, chose to identify himself with our plight and affliction . . . Christ not only pays the penalty for sin, but he does more than the law requires: he accepts the sinner unto himself, adopting that person into his family as a brother or sister. He gives sinners a writ of pardon and embraces them as a loving shepherd who has found the lost sheep.[70]

"Remember that at that time you were separate from Christ, . . . without hope and without God in the world. But now in Christ Jesus you who once were far away have been brought near by the blood of Christ" (Ephesians 2:12-13).

Atonement, redemption, justification, and reconciliation can be seen as opposing ideas about what Jesus' death accomplished, but it is perhaps best to view them as complementary aspects or facets of the complex work of the cross. Through His death and resurrection, Jesus paid the penalty for our sin (atonement), freed us from our bondage to sin (redemption), declared us innocent before God (justification), and brought us into a right relationship with God (reconciliation).

Other views have been expressed about the work of the cross which do not find significant support within the Bible or traditional theology, including:

The Moral Influence Theory: This theory suggests there is no required penalty or repayment for human sin. Rather, God simply demonstrated His love for us by identifying with our sufferings through Jesus' life and His death by crucifixion. His awful death was designed to elicit from us a response of gratitude and obedience so we could live better lives pleasing to God.

The Example Theory: This theory also suggests that no penalty or repayment is required for sin. It holds that Christ's death was an example of total obedience at any cost which demonstrates to us how we should obey God.

Each of these theories rests on an argument that humans can earn their own salvation by either remaining sinless or by living a life that is mostly good and in accordance with God's laws. These ideas are far outside the central Christian teaching that "all have sinned and fall short of the glory of God" (Romans 3:23) and that "salvation is found in no one else, for there is no other name under heaven given to mankind by which we must be saved" (Acts 4:12).

THE REACH OF THE CROSS

While most Christians agree that the death and resurrection of Jesus play a crucial role in the work of salvation from sin, there is disagreement about who benefits from that work. When the Bible says Jesus "is the atoning sacrifice for our sins, and not only for ours but also for the sins of the whole world" (1 John 2:2), what does that mean? There are at least five different arguments about who has benefitted (or can benefit) from the atonement of the cross.

Only the Elect: The most limited view is that Jesus' death achieved atonement only for those people who were chosen beforehand by God through election, also called predestination. In this argument, to say Jesus died for "the whole world" means He died for a chosen few from all nations and all classes. The position takes the belief that salvation is by grace and not works to its furthest reach because no work is involved at all, not even the act of receiving salvation by faith (see Romans 11:5-6).

Those Who Believe: Another view is that Jesus' death provided the opportunity for atonement to every person in the world, but only those who receive the gift of salvation by faith gain any benefit from it. This argument agrees with the first that only a few people are saved by Jesus' work of atonement, but it places the choice of who will receive that gift in the hands of humans exercising free will instead of (or in concert with) God exercising His sovereignty.

For All in Part, For Some in Full: Many theologians agree with the idea that only some receive the full benefit of atonement by freely accepting God's gift of grace, but they believe Jesus' work on the cross benefited all of mankind through what is called general redemption. There are different ways to express this view, but the simplest is to say that Jesus died to pay the penalty for the sins of all, but some people are still lost because they refuse to accept God's offer of forgiveness for their sins. Another way to phrase the argument is that Jesus' death paid the full penalty for Adam's sin, which we inherited from birth. All people are freed from Adam's guilt, but we still must pay the penalty for our own sins unless we personally accept Jesus' atonement for those sins.

All Means All: Others believe that all humans benefit from Christ's defeat of sin at the cross. Two very different ways to reach this conclusion are (1) to believe that God's grace and forgiveness extend to all regardless of their personal faith (i.e., "all roads lead to heaven") or (2) to believe that God will continue to offer grace and forgiveness even after death until all people eventually turn to Him in faith. According to this last belief, hell is not an eternal destination, but a temporary jail cell designed to convince sinners of their need for God.

Creation is Redeemed: Still another way to look at the work of the cross focuses on the restoration of creation rather than the salvation of mankind. While many Christians believe in the ultimate restoration of the earth to God's original plan, some see it as God's primary goal—making individual salvation a matter of secondary importance or even irrelevance. In this view, Jesus' death and resurrection can be seen as a turning point in the battle to "liberate creation from its bondage to decay" (Romans 8:21, paraphrased). Whether through general grace bestowed on the world after Jesus' sacrificial death or through the work of Christians redeemed by faith in Jesus, all of creation will eventually benefit from the coming of God's Kingdom, where God's will shall be done "on earth as it is in heaven" (Matthew 6:10).

THE FINALITY OF THE CROSS

As I stated above, the ultimate climax of a story is that point of decision and action which will ensure a victory or leave the protagonist's goal forever out of reach. The final thing we need to explore about the cross is whether it accomplished this great task of permanently tipping the scales or if it merely served as one of many high points in God's master story—with the ultimate climax yet to come.

It's easy to get confused here because we can mistake the happy celebration at the end of a book or movie for its climax. After all, that's the moment we've been waiting for when the hero of the story stands proudly before the cheering crowd receiving his reward (picture Luke Skywalker and Han Solo at the end of *Star Wars: A New Hope*). But the *climax* is not the celebration at the end of the story. It's an earlier event that makes the celebration possible (Luke shooting his proton torpedoes into an exhaust port on the Death Star causing it to explode).

There are really two options here regarding the finality of the cross. Either Jesus' death and resurrection did all that was needed to defeat sin and Satan and secure a happy ending at the end of the story—or it didn't. Either the triumphant reign of Christ in heaven and earth is a future certainty—or it isn't. Either the cross and the empty tomb marked the ultimate climax of the story, or there is more to be done before victory can be assured.

What we believe about the role of each character—God, the Church, you, and me—*in this chapter of the story* rests on how we view the finality of the work of the cross. This is true of the larger master story, and it's true of our own stories and how we view our personal salvation. We're going to explore this more in the next chapter when we finally come to the end of God's master story.

YOUR TURN

The Bible tells us, "For it is by grace you have been saved, through faith—and this is not from yourselves, it is the gift of God—not by works, so that no one can boast" (Ephesians 2:8-9). In your own words, what do you think it means to be "saved"? What have you been saved from? What have you been saved for?

_____

_____

_____

_____

_____

_____

_____

_____

Go back to the options listed under "The Reach of the Cross" on pages 110-112. Look at the statement of faith or beliefs of your church or school and see if you can tell which of these beliefs it supports. Write it here:_____

_____

_____

_____

_____

_____

_____

11

RESOLUTION

As our story comes to an end, we've experienced . . .

- Exposition—the way things were;
- Inciting incident—what went wrong;
- Rising and falling action as the characters try to achieve their goals and right what's wrong; and
- The ultimate climax where the protagonist acts decisively to assure victory or seal his defeat.

Before the credits roll or we reach the last page of the book, we get to enjoy the *resolution*, or, as the French say it, the *denouement* (day-new-mon), which literally means "the untying":

> The denouement is the final outcome of the story, generally occurring after the climax of the plot. Often it's where all the secrets (if there are any) are revealed and loose ends are tied up . . . As a writer, it's important to keep this in mind when crafting your own story. While you want to give away bits of information about your plot (and subplots) throughout, you want to save the juiciest revelations for the end, rewarding readers for staying the course. That's the ultimate goal of any good denouement.[71]

Other purposes of the resolution are to celebrate victories or mourn defeats, underscore lessons learned by the main characters, resolve any subplots that cropped up during the story, and provide hope for the future.

See if you can match these stories with a summary of their resolution: (For a bonus, can you tell what purpose each resolution fills?)*

___ *The Boys in the Boat*

___ *Holes*

___ *Hamlet*

___ *Gone with the Wind*

___ *The Sixth Sense*

A. The entire royal family is dead. The prince is removed from the scene with all the ceremony of a fallen soldier.

B. After helping a young patient accept his ability to see and talk to dead people, Dr. Crowe discovers that he is also dead and has been through most of the story.

C. After the 1936 Olympics, Joe marries his sweetheart. His teammates go on to successful careers, and many stay close friends for the rest of their lives.

D. The Yelnats family curse is lifted, Hector is reunited with his mother, and Camp Green Lake becomes a Girl Scout Camp.

E. Scarlett decides to return to Tara, her family home, remembering that "tomorrow is another day."

CELEBRATING THE VICTORY

One of the hallmarks of Christianity is the hope for a future in which sin, death, evil, and sorrow have been defeated. We look forward to a day when God "will wipe every tear from [our] eyes. There will be no more death or mourning or crying or pain, for the old order of things has passed away" (Revelation 21:4). However, Christians differ widely in their understanding of what is still to come before we can celebrate that eternal victory.

---

* The answers can be found at the end of the chapter.

Much of this disagreement centers on the book of Revelation, the last book of the Bible. Some Christians believe the book is mostly prophetic, explaining what will happen in the future during the "end times" of our earth in its present form. Others believe the book does not contain actual prophecy but was written about events that happened during the first century after Jesus' death and resurrection. It's not just the words of Revelation under scrutiny, but also prophecies contained in the Old Testament books of Daniel, Ezekiel, Jeremiah, and Zechariah and the words of Jesus and Paul in the New Testament which may point to a future fulfillment.

Most Christians do believe Jesus will return to earth at some point in the future. There are three main thoughts on the timing of that great day.

Premillennialism: The term "premillennial" refers to a belief that the second coming of Jesus Christ to the earth will occur *before* a millennial period described in Revelation 20 and *directly after* the Great Tribulation described in Revelation 6-18. Most who adhere to this view believe there will be a literal 1,000-year time period (a millennium) when Jesus will personally live on the earth and rule over all the nations of the world. Satan will literally be bound and unable to deceive the inhabitants of the world until the end of the 1,000 years.

In his book on Revelation, Steve Gregg provides this summary of premillennialism:

> Christ will reign with his saints here on earth prior to the establishment of the eternal new heavens and new earth. The millennial reign will be characterized by international peace and justice resulting from the universal enforced rule of Christ over saved and unsaved alike. At the end of this time, Satan's brief period of freedom will put humanity to one final test just before the final judgment.[72]

There is much debate about the events of the Great Tribulation (Matthew 24:21-22; Revelation 7:14) and whether Christians will live through this horrible time or be raptured before it begins (supernaturally snatched up from the earth to meet Jesus in the sky) (1 Thessalonians 4:16-17). There is also debate about who will reign with Jesus in the millennial kingdom.

Postmillennialism: Another view is that the millennial kingdom of Revelation 20 refers to a real historical period that will *precede* the second coming of Jesus to earth. It may refer to a specific time period in the future, or it could refer to the full length of time following Jesus' return to heaven as the Kingdom of God has spread around the world (giving 1,000 years a symbolic rather than a literal meaning). In this view, the Great Tribulation spoken of by Jesus and the author of Revelation is seen as a past event, probably the destruction of Jerusalem and the Temple in 70 AD and the dispersion of the Jewish people out of Judea, and only the final two chapters of Revelation remain as future events.

Most Christians in this group believe Jesus will return to earth to usher in a final judgment (Revelation 20:7-15) and "a new heaven and a new earth" (Revelation 21:1) but only after the requirements of the millennial period are fulfilled.

As described by Gregg:

> The 1,000 years of peace will be accomplished through no other agency than that which is already in possession of the church, i.e. the Word of God and the Holy Spirit. The world will become Christianized, either as the result of worldwide revival and mass conversions, or through the imposition of Christian ideals by converted rulers and Christian governments—or both.[73]

Amillennialism: Augustine of Hippo was one of the early church fathers who discarded the idea of a literal millennial kingdom and became an amillennialist (no millennium). In this view, the battles and tribulation throughout Revelation are usually seen as symbolic references to the ongoing spiritual struggle between God's people and the forces of evil. The millennial kingdom of Revelation 20 is believed to refer to the entire Church age, the time between Jesus' ascension to heaven and the end of time. Some who hold this view believe that Jesus already "returned" to judge Israel in 70 AD and has continued to be "present" in the lives of believers ever since. Others expect Jesus to come again at the end of the world to usher in a final judgment and a new earth.

One thing I have learned in my study of Revelation is that there are many theories and little agreement about what will happen in our future. Quite a few theories have already been proved false as the dates some have predicted for Jesus' return have come and gone. It shouldn't surprise us there is so much debate about the timing of Jesus' return or other possible unfulfilled prophecies in the Bible. It's as if we had all been reading a thrilling suspense story and had the book ripped from our hands before we could read the last chapter. We might be able to calmly discuss the setting of the story and the goals of the different characters, but we all clamor to know how the story ends.

Whether Christians believe in premillennialism, postmillennialism, or amillennialism, it is possible for them to think of Jesus' work on the cross as the ultimate defeat of evil and the climax of God's master story. Whatever awaits in our future, the final victory of Jesus and His reign on earth (in person or through the Church or the Christian community) is assured. But not all Christians are convinced on this point. Much of the talk you hear from Christians in the public sphere is about the need to win the war against our evil culture or the need to restore God's broken creation, as if the final climax of the story is still in the future and is up to us. It's important, then, that we understand what we really believe about these things so our role in the master story will be clear.

WRAPPING UP THE SUBPLOTS

Another purpose of a story's resolution is to show what happened to all the characters in the story and to wrap up any subplots. God's master story has had many characters and many subplots. Some have ended as the story progressed and others will not be fully completed or understood until the end. The fate of nations, the role of other religions and ideologies, and the eternal destiny of each individual human who ever lived are all important parts of the story.

Many Christians use the word "salvation" when discussing the eternal destiny (or destination) of each human. People who are "saved" are promised eternal life and will be raised with Jesus on the "last day" (John 6:40).

There are, in general, three opposing beliefs among Christians about salvation:

1. Salvation is by faith alone and cannot be lost (see, John 6:37-39; 2 Corinthians 1:21-22, Hebrews 9:12).

2. Salvation is by faith but a person can fall from grace and lose their salvation if they do not continue in their faith (see Matthew 10:22; John 15:6; 2 Timothy 2:12; Hebrews 6:4-6).

3. Salvation is made possible by the cross, but it is obtained by faith and good works, including for some participating in the sacraments of their church (see Matthew 25:31-46; James 2:14-26; Revelation 20:12).

For those who believe in the permanence of salvation (option #1), their personal acceptance of Jesus' atonement for sins marks the great climax of their story subplot. Victory (in this case, eternal life with Jesus) is assured! For those who believe in options #2 and #3, victory is made possible by what Jesus did on the cross, but they can't be certain of obtaining that victory until their lives are over and they face God's judgment. For them, the climax of the story may be the moment of judgment when they learn their eternal fate.

In your own personal story, which of these do you think is true?

[ ] Jesus atoned for all my sins, past and future. I have accepted this gift of grace, and there is nothing else I have to do to be saved.

[ ] Jesus atoned for my sins, allowing me to begin a process of justification through faith, church membership, and good works.

[ ] Jesus atoned for my sins, but I can lose my salvation if I don't live right.

[ ] Other:_____

_____

_____

LEARNING THE LESSONS

While judgment for some will bring eternal life with Jesus, what will happen to those who have rejected Jesus or who never even knew about Him? There are several views on this topic as well:

(1) The *exclusive* view is that a person can only be saved by hearing the gospel of Jesus' death and resurrection and accepting His offer of redemption. This view is sometimes expanded by including those before the time of Jesus who believed in God and had faith that He would provide atonement for their sins (such as the Old Testament patriarchs).

(2) The *inclusive* view is "that non-Christians can achieve salvation by somehow believing and acting as Christians without realizing it," although this is usually limited to someone who "has not heard the gospel but is longing for something like it."[74]

(3) The *pluralist* view opens salvation to any number of non-Christians who have simply lived good lives (and is the furthest view from mainstream Christianity).

What about those who have intentionally rejected the message of the cross or have lived lives in defiance of God's call for righteousness and repentance? According to different views, they will be consigned to the eternal torments of hell, they will have other opportunities after death to repent, or they will simply cease to exist when they die.

Although exclusivism is the traditional belief of Christian theologians, the last two options have had proponents throughout Christian history.

These different ideas highlight the tension between two of the most important lessons taught throughout the Bible: (1) that God is loving and merciful and (2) that God is holy and just. What is important is that we, as Christians, do not base our belief about the eternal destiny of unbelievers on our personal wishes or a few verses of the Bible taken out of context. The ideas of *universalism* and *pluralism* fit well into our modern multicultural societies, where intolerance and exclusivism are condemned as the enemies of peace among men. But they may not fit well into a Christian worldview based on the teachings of the Bible, where peace with God is built on a foundation of repentance and righteousness.

REVEALING THE SECRETS

For me, the best part about finally reaching the end of God's master story is that so many of the mysteries of the Bible and of life in general will finally be made clear. We'll finally have the answers to the questions Christians have grappled with for the last 2,000 years. How can God be three persons but one essence? How did God create the world, and how long did it take? Was there a worldwide flood, and, if so, where did Noah's Ark land? When Jesus was a little boy, did He know He was divine? What's the full story about Mary and Joseph and the many other people in the Bible we only read a bit about?

As we look around us in our resurrected bodies we will finally know if we are in a completely new setting or in a redeemed version of our current planet. We will see if our friends and family members are there (and possibly our beloved pets). And we will learn what new purpose God has for us as we enter into an eternal existence.

Before that great day, though, there will be many things we simply cannot be sure of—and I think God planned it that way. Why? Because He wants us to trust Him. He wants us to turn to Him with our questions and have faith that He knows the answers even if we never do.

Theologian Richard Mouw writes:

The Christian life is all about trust in the promises of a personal God, a sovereign Ruler who assures us of the ultimate victory over all that oppresses us. We can face the future with a basic confidence, not because we have been provided with a special collection of secret facts about what is to come, but because we have been allowed by grace to enter into a relationship with the Lord of the future.[75]

This attitude of faith and trust is much easier if we each understand what we really believe about God's master story and our part in it. By examining each part of the story and basing our beliefs on God's Word instead of our own wishful thinking, popular opinion, or whatever we hear from our favorite pastor or teacher, we can have an unshakable hope that the story will end just as the author intends—and it will be good!

YOUR TURN

I love old hymns and songs about the hope we have for a new life after our present lives on earth are over. My favorite is "Revelation Song" by Philips, Craig and Dean. What are some of your favorites?_____

_____

_____

What is the one question you would most like to learn the answer to when you reach heaven or the new earth?_____

_____

_____

What is a silly or unimportant question you would like to learn the answer to?

_____

_____

_____

Now for a hard question. Are you confident that your own part in the master story will turn out well in the end? Why, or why not?_____

_____

_____

_____

_____

_____

_____

_____

_____

_____

_____

_____

_____

_____

_____

_____

_____

THE CHAPTER CHALLENGE

As you can see, resolutions can be happy or sad. The answers to the matching game at the beginning of this chapter are: (A) *Hamlet,* (B) *The Sixth Sense,* (C) *The Boys in the Boat,* (D) *Holes,* and (E) *Gone with the Wind.*

THE WHOLE STORY

12

So, have you got it all figured out?

Do you know exactly what you believe about each part of God's master story?

I would be surprised if you answered "yes." I know I don't have it all figured out, and I'm sure I never will. I'm looking forward to reaching the end of the story and being surprised and delighted by all the new things I'm going to learn about God and His creation. But that doesn't stop me from asking questions and searching for answers now. Why? Because what I believe now determines how I will live my life—this one life I've been given—this one chance I have to be a part of this present story.

As we discussed earlier in this book, everyone has a worldview, a set of deeply held beliefs about the existence of God and the nature of reality, the world, and our place in it. We don't get to wait until the story is over to decide what we think about it. We're living in it now. If I don't want my worldview to be based on falsehoods, half-truths, and wishful thinking, I need to carefully consider my beliefs and develop my worldview intentionally. I need to understand what I believe and why I believe it.

THE SEARCH FOR TRUTH

Okay, so everyone has a worldview. How can I know that my worldview is the right one—that what I believe is true?

Truth is a tough word these days. We live in an age when many people are dismissing the idea of absolute truth and substituting it with relative truth. *What is true for you may not be true for me. I have no right to judge what others believe. There is no objective truth. You do you!* These are the claims and slogans of the 21st century. In 2016, Oxford Dictionaries selected "post-truth" as its Word of the Year, defining the term as "relating to or denoting circumstances in which objective facts are less influential in shaping public opinion than appeals to emotion and personal belief."[76] Ten years earlier, the Word of the Year had been "truthiness"—"believing something that feels true, even if it isn't supported by fact."[77] Truth, facts, even reality have become dirty words. So the only thing that matters is that I'm comfortable with my own worldview—right?

Wrong.

Perhaps the most important belief of Christianity is that there is a God—one God. He is the creator and sovereign of the universe. He is the *author* of the whole story of the universe. He defines what is true. Another important belief of Christianity is that humans are not God. We never were and we never will be. The first sin recorded in the Bible—the inciting incident that started all the trouble—is when Adam and Eve wanted to become like God (Genesis 3:1-7). Instead of trusting what God told them, the first humans wanted to understand reality on their own terms. But the crafty serpent had lied to them. (Sorry, he gave them "alternative facts" to create "post-truth" so they could rely on "truthiness" instead of truth.) Instead of becoming like God, Adam and Eve were estranged from God, learning the difference between good and evil by experiencing evil firsthand.

Truth exists because God exists. Reality is what it is, not what we want it to be or exactly what we perceive it to be. Truth defines us, not the other way around. The goal of every person, and especially Christians, should be to align our personal worldview with the external truth about our world to the best of our ability. Only then can we come close to accurately answering the big questions of life and understanding our role in the master story.

Following this chapter, you will find a place to write out what you believe about the major elements of God's master story as you now understand it. Who's moving the story forward? What are their goals? What went wrong with our world, what is God doing to fix it, and what is our role in the story? Before you turn there, I want us to explore two more questions regarding credibility and diversity. First, how can we be sure our personal views of what God is doing in the world are credible—that they are most likely true? Second, is it a good thing or a bad thing that Christians have different beliefs about the bigger story we are all in?

TESTS FOR TRUTH

In their book, *Worlds Apart: A Handbook on World Views*, Norman Geisler and William Watson set out several tests for the credibility of a worldview. They were writing about primary worldviews like theism, deism, atheism, and pantheism, but two of their tests can be useful in sorting through our personal worldviews as well:

"A world view must be consistent."[78]

As McKee says: "A beautifully told story is a symphonic unity in which structure, setting, character, genre, and idea meld seamlessly. To find their harmony, the writer must study the elements of story as if they were instruments of an orchestra—first separately, then in concert."[79] In the same way, we need to study our beliefs about the different elements of God's master story and make sure they work together as a consistent whole. As you write out your beliefs about the different elements of God's master story at the end of this book, ask yourself if they are consistent with each other.

Do you believe in the miracles of Jesus' incarnation and resurrection but not the miracle of creation? Do you believe the Bible was divinely inspired, but you don't consider it an authority for the choices you make in your life? Do you believe that people are only saved by personal faith in Jesus, but you're more concerned with getting people to obey God's laws than accept God's grace? Or do you believe we need to transform our cultures, but you think it's best not to talk about your beliefs? These are the kinds of questions you will need to ask yourself if you want to have a credible worldview. If you are holding beliefs that are contradictory, at least one of those beliefs is most likely false.

"A world view must be comprehensive."[80]

Many Christians think about their beliefs one at a time. We study various religious doctrines separately and put a checkmark next to the view we think is most likely true. But a worldview is more than a collection of doctrines or a chapter of a book—it's the whole story! Geisler and Watkins explain that "[a] worldview should cover the whole world of reality. It must encompass all of man's experience. If a world view is putting the whole picture together, it must use all the pieces."[81]

Ravi Zacharias and Vince Vitale suggest that a credible worldview must answer four questions: "Origin—Where did I come from? Meaning—Why am I here? Morality—How should I live? Destiny—Where am I headed?"[82] If you refuse to define your beliefs about important things like how the world began, what went wrong, and where we're all headed, your worldview is incomplete. You can't intentionally live out God's plan for your life if you don't understand the greater story you are part of.

Having a consistent and comprehensive worldview provides us with a clear understanding of the world we live in and helps us make decisions about how we should live. It also makes our witness to the world much stronger. It's very difficult to tell others about Jesus and His plan of salvation if we don't understand it ourselves. And no matter how well-rehearsed we are in explaining our Christian beliefs to non-believers, if our words say one thing and our actions say something else, no one is going to believe us!

I would like to add one more test for the credibility of a worldview:

A Christian worldview must be biblical.

In addition to being internally consistent and comprehensive, a credible worldview needs to be based on something that is itself verifiable and authoritative. For Christians, the foundation of our beliefs has to be the Bible. If God really exists, if He made us with a purpose, if He sent His Son into the world to remedy our separation from Him, then He has surely communicated with us in a way we can understand. He has given us a written word to guide us to know Him better and follow Him better. It may not answer all our questions, but it's the place we need to start to develop a worldview that is not only credible but is *Christian*.

DIFFERENT VIEWS OF THE TRUTH

Another major belief of Christianity is that we are not in this alone. We are part of a Christian community with members all around the world. We are the Church.

New Testament writers sometimes referred to a church or a collection of churches, by which they meant a group of Christians meeting together in a local place. Other times they referred to the Church as a single entity comprising all Christians everywhere.*

The Bible compares the Church to a living body, with Jesus as the head and the rest of us as eyes, ears, hands, and feet (1 Corinthians 12:12-27). It is also compared to a building, a single structure made up of many parts (1 Corinthians 3:9; Ephesians 2:19-22). Each Christian has the task of adding to that building as he is able, with "gold, silver, costly stones, wood, hay or straw" (1 Corinthians 3:10-12). Some of what we build will last, while other parts will be destroyed because we didn't build it carefully enough (1 Corinthians 3:12-15).

Looking at the state of Christianity today, it's hard to see how we are all working together as members of one body, building something together. There seems to be more diversity than unity in the Church, with its wide array of denominations and doctrines. Shouldn't we all try to get along

---

*   Today, most writers capitalize "Church" to mean all Christians and use the non-capitalized "church" to mean a local gathering or a building, but most Bible translations use "church" for both meanings.

and come up with one set of doctrines and beliefs we can all agree on? In his book, *Christ and Culture*, H. Richard Niebuhr concludes with a caution against trying to identify a single way to define Christianity and Christian beliefs. The question of how to live in our world as a Christian "is by no means a new one, . . . the problem has been an enduring one through all the Christian centuries."[83] But the full and final answer to the question is not ours to give.

As Niebuhr says:

> We should need to assume, if we tried to give *the* Christian answer, that we are representatives of the head of the church, not members of the body, that we represent its reason rather than being subject to it as hands or feet, ears or eyes, arthritic fingers or stiffened joints.[84]

Niebuhr compared the work of Christianity to a great battle, with the overall strategy "in the mind of the Captain rather than of any lieutenants."[85] But if we are to be engaged in that battle, we need to understand our part of it. Each Christian must come to their own "final conclusion" about the big questions in life "in resolutions that involve a leap from the chair in which he has read about ancient battles into the middle of a present conflict."[86]

C.S. Lewis arrived at a similar conclusion in his book, *Mere Christianity*. Attempting to set forth the basic beliefs all Christians share, Lewis described Christianity as a house with many rooms. Rather than suggesting we all leave our rooms (our particular church, denomination, or worldview) and join each other in the hall, he thought we each needed to commit to specific beliefs about God, the world, and ourselves, even if those beliefs differed:

> [Christianity] is more like a hall out of which doors open into several rooms . . . But it is in the rooms, not in the hall, that there are fires and chairs and meals. The hall is a place to wait in, a place from which to try the various doors, not a place to live in. For that purpose the worst of the rooms (whichever that may

be) is, I think, preferable. It is true that some people may have to wait in the hall for a considerable time, while others feel certain almost at once which door they must knock at . . . But you must regard it as waiting, not camping. You must keep on praying for light: and, of course, even in the hall you must begin trying to obey the rules which are common to the whole house. And above all you must be asking which door is the true one; not which pleases you best by its paint and paneling. In plain language, the question should never be: "Do I like that kind of service?" but "Are these doctrines true: Is holiness here?"[87]

John Piper agreed with Lewis when he wrote:

For many years my conviction has been that Christian unity and Christian truth are served best not by removing fences, but by loving across them and having welcoming gates . . . The point is that minimizing truth, or filing down its clear edges, or blending it all into one indistinguishable mass, or focusing on prayer, service, and mission, rather than truth — none of these produces unity that honors truth, creates robust communities, or endures for generations.

That happens best when we live well in our communities of conviction, and love well across convictional lines . . . What the world needs from the great house of Christianity is not that all the walls be knocked out between the rooms, but that we love each other in all the ways the Bible says, including defending and confirming the truth of Scripture as we see it (Ephesians 4:15).[88]

THE SOURCE OF TRUTH

The simple fact is that Christians in different churches and denominations see things differently when it comes to where we came from, what went wrong, what God is doing to fix it, and how we are to help in that great mission. But we have more in common than we might think. One important thing we share is hope. Hope for ourselves. Hope for our world. Hope for a better end to our story than we can now imagine. This uniquely Christian hope doesn't come from knowing the whole of God's story from the beginning to the end. It comes from knowing the Author.

In the book of Job in the Old Testament, many questions are asked about why God allows pain and suffering and why He doesn't make everything right *right now*. Job, who suffered as much as any person can, felt he was being punished unfairly by God. He ended his questioning: "Oh, that I had someone to hear me! I sign now my defense—let the Almighty answer me" (Job 31:35). And God did answer—in His own way. Instead of answering any of Job's "why" questions, God reminded Job of His sovereignty over all of creation in these excerpts from Job 38:

> *Where were you when I laid the earth's foundation?*
>
> *Tell me, if you understand . . .*
>
> *Have you ever given orders to the morning,*
>
> *or shown the dawn its place? . . .*
>
> *Have you journeyed to the springs of the sea*
>
> *or walked in the recesses of the deep? . . .*
>
> *Can you raise your voice to the clouds*
>
> *and cover yourself with a flood of water?*
>
> *Do you send the lightning bolts on their way?*
>
> *Do they report to you, 'Here we are'?*

The fact that God has not provided answers to all our questions is not a reason to stop believing in Him or to stop hoping for a better future. It is a reason to examine our beliefs about God and work on getting to know Him in a deeper, more personal way. If we allow our personal relationship with God and our continual study of His word to shape our worldview, we can't fail to find our own part in God's master story.

YOUR TURN

Imagine for a moment walking into a Broadway theater in the middle of a live show. The people on stage are talking about some big event you didn't see, or they're running around trying to prevent some catastrophe you don't know anything about. Now imagine getting pulled onto the stage to perform as one of the characters in the play—without a script! Well, you're in this story now—God's master story—and it's time to play your part.

It's not a story about you, even though you will experience the story from your own unique perspective. And it's not just a story about getting saved and going to heaven or being resurrected to a new life on a new earth. It's a story about God working in the world today and calling His people to work alongside Him to accomplish His goals and bring the story to an amazing end.

Let me leave you with one more movie quote: "Everything will be all right in the end . . . If it's not all right, then it's not yet the end."[89]

It's not yet the end.

Go, play your part!

GOD'S MASTER STORY SYNOPSIS

Questions to get you started:

> Who is the author of the story?

> Who is telling the story (from whose perspective is the story told)?

> Is there one or more than one storyteller?

Exposition:

> Describe the setting "in the beginning."

Inciting Incident:

What went wrong?

Who were the major characters at this point in the story? Include protagonists and antagonists.

Describe the setting after the inciting incident:

Rising Action:

Characters:	Goal:

Obstacles and Opposition:

Climax: can be the ultimate climax or an act one or two climax:

What did Jesus accomplish?

Describe the setting today:

Have any of the characters or goals changed?

Action still to come:

Resolution:

In the present, what do you think God is doing to work toward His goal?

How does He want us to help Him in His mission?

What are two or three specific things you can do to help?

THE NICENE CREED

FIRST COUNCIL OF NICEA, 325 A.D.

We believe in one God, the Father, the almighty, the maker of all things seen and unseen.

And in one Lord Jesus Christ, the Son of God; begotten from the Father; only-begotten – that is, from the substance of the Father; God from God; light from light; true God from true God; begotten not made; being of one substance with the Father; through whom all things in heaven and on earth came into being; who on account of us human beings and our salvation came down and took flesh, becoming a human being; he suffered and rose again on the third day, ascended into the heavens; and will come again to judge the living and the dead.

And in the Holy Spirit.[90]

NOTES

CREATIVE WORKS CITED

SONGS:

Phillips, Craig & Dean. "Revelation Song." *Fearless*, INO, 2009.

MOVIES:

Apollo 13. Directed by Ron Howard, Universal, 1995.

The Avengers. Directed by Joss Whedon, Marvel, 2012.

The Best Exotic Marigold Hotel. Directed by John Madden, Fox Searchlight, 2011.

Casablanca. Directed by Michael Curtiz, Warner Bros., 1942.

Cinderella. Directed by Clyde Geronimi, Hamilton Luske, and Wilfred Jackson, Disney, 1950.

Cowboys & Aliens. Directed by Jon Favreau, Universal and DreamWorks, 2011.

Die Hard. Directed by John McTiernan, 20th Century Fox, 1988.

Dr. Strange. Directed by Scott Derrickson, Marvel, 2016.

Gnomeo and Juliet. Directed by Kelly Asbury, Disney and Touchstone Pictures, 2011.

Gone with the Wind. Directed by Victor Fleming, Selznick International Pictures and Metro-Goldwyn-Mayer, 1939.

Harry Potter and the Sorcerer's Stone. Directed by Chris Columbus, Warner Bros., 2001.

Hoodwinked. Directed by Cory Edwards and Todd Edwards, The Weinstein Company, 2005.

Indiana Jones: Raiders of the Lost Ark. Directed by Steven Spielberg, Paramount Pictures, 1981.

It's a Wonderful Life. Directed by Frank Capra, RKO Radio Pictures, 1946.

Jurassic World. Directed by Colin Trevorrow, Universal, 2015.

Mission Impossible – Fallout. Directed by Christopher McQuarrie, Paramount, 2018.

North by Northwest. Directed by Alfred Hitchcock, Metro-Goldwyn-Mayer, 1959.

Pizza My Heart. Directed by Andy Wolk, ABC Family, 2005.

The Poseidon Adventure. Directed by Ronald Neam, 20th Century Fox, 1972.

Saving Private Ryan. Directed by Steven Spielberg, DreamWorks, 1998.

Serendipity. Directed by Peter Chelsom, Miramax Film, 2001.

The Sixth Sense. Directed by M. Night Shyamalan, Buena Vista Pictures, 1999.

Star Wars Episode V: The Empire Strikes Back. Directed by Irvin Kershner, Lucasfilm, 1980.

Star Wars Episode IV: A New Hope. Directed by George Lucas, Lucasfilm, 1977.

Top Gun. Directed by Tony Scott, Paramount, 1986.

Toy Story. Directed by John Lasseter, Pixar, 1995.

West Side Story. Directed by Robert Wise and Jerome Robbins, United Artists, 1961.

The Wizard of Oz. Directed by Victor Fleming, Metro-Goldwyn-Mayer, 1939.

Wreck-It Ralph. Directed by Rich Moore, Disney, 2012.

You've Got Mail. Directed by Nora Ephron, Warner Bros., 1998.

BOOKS: (WITH ORIGINAL PUBLICATION INFORMATION)

Austen, Jane. *Pride and Prejudice*. T. Egerton, Whitehall, 1813.

Brown, Daniel James. *The Boys in the Boat*. Penguin, 2013.

Card, Orson Scott. *Ender's Game*. Tor Books, 1985.

Collins, Suzanne. *The Hunger Games*. Scholastic, 2008.

London, Jack. *The Call of the Wild*. McMillan, 1903.

Milne, A.A. *Winnie the Pooh*. Methuen & Co. Ltd., 1926.

Sachar, Louis. *Holes*. Farrar, Straus and Giroux, 1998.

Shakespeare, William. *Hamlet*. Circa 1600.

Shakespeare, William. *Romeo and Juliet*. Circa 1590.

Stockett, Kathryn. *The Help*. Penguin Books, 2009.

Tolkien, J.R.R. *The Hobbit*. George Allen & Unwin, 1937.

Tolkien, J.R.R. *The Lord of the Rings*. Allen & Unwin, 1954-55.

Tolkien, J.R.R. *The Silmarillion*. Allen & Unwin, 1977.

Verne, Jules. *Around the World in Eighty Days*. Pierre-Jules Hetzel, 1872.

ENDNOTES

1   James W. Sire, *Naming the Elephant: Worldview as a Concept.* 2nd ed., Intervarsity Press, 2015, p. 24.

2   Norman L. Geisler, and William D. Watkins. *Worlds Apart: A Handbook on World Views.* 2nd ed., Wipf and Stock, 2003, pp. 15-17.

3   Geisler and Watkins. [In addition to theism, atheism, pantheism, deism, and polytheism, Geisler and Watkins also include panentheism and finite godism in their discussion of worldviews.]

4   Ravi Zacharias and Vince Vitale. *Jesus Among Secular Gods: The Countercultural Claims of Christ.* Faith Words, 2018. [Zacharias and Vitale include atheism, scientism, pluralism, humanism, relativism, and hedonism in their book on secular worldviews.]

5   For example, Dell Tackett, "What's Your View of the World?" Focus on the Family, 2006. https://www.focusonthefamily.com/faith/christian-worldview/whats-a-christian-worldview/whats-your-view-of-the-world. Retrieved 3 January 2019.

6   Sire, p. 141.

7   Sire, p. 141.

8   *Indiana Jones: Raiders of the Lost Ark.* Directed by Steven Spielberg, Paramount Pictures, 1981.

9   *Star Wars – The Empire Strikes Back.* Directed by Irvin Kershner, Lucasfilm. 1980.

10   "Orthodox." *Oxford Dictionaries.* www.oxforddictionaries.com/us/definition/american _english/orthodox.

11   "Unorthodox." *Oxford Dictionaries.* www.oxforddictionaries.com/us/definition/american _english/unorthodox.

12   *Indiana Jones: Raiders of the Lost Ark.* Directed by Steven Spielberg, Paramount Pictures, 1981.

The Wizard of Oz. Directed by Victor Fleming, Metro-Goldwyn-Mayer, 1939.

Casablanca. Directed by Michael Curtiz, Warner Bros., 1942.

Harry Potter and the Sorcerer's Stone. Directed by Chris Columbus, Warner Bros., Heyday Films, 1492 Pictures, 2001.

Star Wars Episode V - The Empire Strikes Back. Directed by Irvin Kershner, Lucasfilm, 1980.

13   A.A. Milne. *Winnie the Pooh.* Dutton's Children's Books, 1988, p. 4.

J.R.R. Tolkien. *The Hobbit.* Ballantine Books, 1976, p. 15.

Jane Austen. *Pride and Prejudice.* Barnes & Noble, 1993, p. 1.

14   *Hoodwinked.* Directed by Cory Edwards and Todd Edwards, Blue Yonder Films with Kanbar Entertainment, 2005.

15   Robert McKee. *Story: Substance, Structure, Style, and the Principles of Screenwriting.* HarperCollins, 1997, p. 80.

16   Sire, p. 40 (quoting Kok, John H. "Learning to Teach from Within a Christian Perspective," *Pro Rege*, June 2003, 12).

17   Sire, p. 141.

18   Sire, p. 145.

19   "Presupposition."   *Dictionary.com.*   www.dictionary.com/browse/presupposition?s=t.

20   Jane Austen. *Pride and Prejudice.* Barnes & Noble, 1993, p. 1.

21   Henry Blackaby, et al. *Experiencing God: Knowing and Doing the Will of God.* Revised and expanded, B&H Publishing, 2008, p. 10.

22   Kathryn Stockett, *The Help.* Berkeley Publishing Group, 2009, p. 1.

23   Orson Scott Card, *Ender's Game.* Tom Doherty Associates, 1994, pp. 289-290.

24   J.R.R. Tolkien, *The Lord of the Rings: Part Two, The Two Towers,* Ballantine Books, 1966, p. 363.

25   John R.W. Stott, "The Doctrine of Scripture." *The Portable Seminary,* edited by David Horton, Bethany House, 2006, p. 23.

26   Charles C Ryrie, *Basic Theology,* Moody Press, 1999, p. 81.

27 "U.S. Public Becoming Less Religious." *Pew Research Center,* November 3, 2015, www.pewforum.org/2015/11/03/u-s-public-becoming-less-religious.

28 Kate Shellnut, "Just Give Me Jesus: A Closer Look at Christians Who Don't Go to Church." *Christianity Today,* April 7, 1917, www.christianitytoday. com/gleanings/2017/april/love-jesus-not-church-barna-spiritual-but-notreligious.html.

29 "The Nicene Creed." *The Christian Theology Reader,* 4th Ed., edited by in Alister E. McGrath, Wiley-Blackwell, 2011, p. 9.

30 Suzanne Collins, *The Hunger Games.* Scholastic, 2008, pp. 4-5.

31 H. Richard Nieburh, *Christ & Culture.* Harper One, 2001, p. 32.

32 Niebuhr, p. 83.

33 Niebuhr, p. 136.

34 Niebuhr, p. 149.

35 "The Nicene Creed."

36 Not everyone agrees with the idea of the Trinity. For example, the Apostolic Church, which considers itself to be Christian, teaches there is only one God who has manifested Himself in different ways throughout history. "Constitution of the Apostolic Assembly of the Faith in Christ Jesus." 2007, apps. apostolicassembly.org/downloads/Constitution07Eng.pdf, p. 100.

37 Scott Richert, "What is a saint?" March 7, 2017, www.thoughtco.com/what-is-a-saint-542857.

38 Robert G. Clouse, "The Doctrine of the Church." *The Portable Seminary,* edited by David Horton. Bethany House, 2006, p. 182.

39 Don Fleming, *The AMG Concise Bible Commentary.* AMG. 1994, p. 11.

40 Augustine of Hippo, *Confessions,* Book XIII (circa 397).

41 Augustine of Hippo, *The City of God,* Book XI, Chapter 9 (circa 400).

42 Augustine of Hippo, *The Literal Meaning of Genesis* (401).

43 McKee, p. 181.

44 McKee, p. 192.

45 What is an Inciting Incident?" *Reference.* www.reference.com/education/inciting-incident-8b86c25c4f2d7d54.

46 *The Westminster Shorter Catechism*, question 19. westminsterconfession.org/confessional-standards/the-westminster-shorter-catechism.php.

47 Stanley J. Grenz, *Theology for the Community of God*. Eerdmans, 2000, pp. 181-182.

48 There are non-traditional answers to this question as well, including the Pelagian view which was condemned as heresy in the fifth century. Pelagianism taught that humans are born innocent and have free will to sin or to remain sinless.

49 The dictionary definition of depraved is "marked by corruption or evil." *Merriam-Webster.* www.merriam-webster.com/dictionary/depraved. In theology, the word is used to indicate that a person's entire nature is marked by sin. It does not mean the person is entirely evil or incapable of good deeds or thoughts.

50 Psalm 143:2; Ecclesiastes 7:20; Romans 3:23; Joseph Pohle, "Pelagius and Pelagianism." *The Catholic Encyclopedia*. Vol. 11. New York: Robert Appleton Company. www.newadvent.org/cathen/11604a.htm, retrieved July 19, 2018.

51 James R. Hull, "Demystifying Plot Points and the Inciting Incident." *Narrative First* (2018). https://narrativefirst.com/articles/plot-points-and-the-inciting-incident, retrieved May 14, 2020.

52 Catechism of the Catholic Church, 2nd ed., *Libreria Editrice Vaticana*, #289. ccc.usccb.org/ flipbooks/catechism/files/assets/basic-html/page-I.html.

53 McKee, p. 192.

54 Hull, para. 2

55 J.R.R. Tolkien, *The Silmarillion*, Del Rey Books: New York, 2002, pp. 109-110.

56 TOW Project, "Genesis 1-11 and Work." Theology of Work. www.theologyofwork.org/old-testament/genesis-1-11-and-work#the-work-of-thecreation-mandate-genesis-128-215 (retrieved 10/4/18)

57 Sire, p. 141

58 Kenneth Boa, "Divine Sovereignty vs. Human Responsibility." *Bible.org.* bible.org/article/divine-sovereignty-vs-human-responsibility.

59 McKee, p. 210.

60 McKee, p. 211.

61 Richard Bremmer as Lord Voldermort. *Harry Potter and the Sorcerer's Stone*. Warner Bros, 2001.

62   Ravi K. Zacharias and Vince Vitale. *Why Suffering?: Finding Meaning and Comfort When Life Doesn't Make Sense.* FaithWords, 2014, p. 56.

63   William C. Placher, *Essentials of Christian Theology,* edited by William C. Placher, Westminster John Knox Press, 2003, p. 98.

64   Penina Taylor, "The Jewish View of Satan." *JewishAnswers.org.* www.jewishanswers.org/ ask-the-rabbi-2566/the-jewish-view-of-satan/?p=2566.

65   Tovia Singer, "Who is Satan?" *Outreach Judaism.* outreachjudaism.org/who-is-satan.

66   Sarah Eekhoff Zylstra, "The Top 50 Countries Where It's Most Dangerous to Follow Jesus." *Christianity Today,* January 10, 2018. www.christianitytoday.com/news/2018/january/top-50-christian-persecution-open-doors-world-watch-list.html.

67   Samuel Dibin, "Mahatma Gandhi and Christianity." *Christian Today,* August 14, 2008. www.christiantoday.co.in/article/mahatma.gandhi.and.christianity/2837.htm.

68   Elizabeth Foster, "Climax in Literature: Definition & Examples." *Study.com.* study.com/academy/lesson/climax-in-literature-definition-examples.html.

69   "What does the Greek word 'tetelestai' mean?" *Bible.org.* bible.org/question/what-does-greek-word-tetelestai-mean.

70   Donald G. Bloesch, "A Biblical View of Sin." *The Portable Seminary,* edited by David Horton, Bethany House, 2006, p. 175.

71   Brian A. Klems, "What is a Denouement?" *WritersDigest.com.* December 4, 2014. https://www.writersdigest.com/online-editor/what-is-a-denouement.

72   Steve Gregg, *Revelation: Four Views, Revised & Updated.* Thomas Nelson, 2013, pp. 46-47.

73   Gregg, p. 517.

74   Placher, p. 300.

75   Richard J. Mouw, "Where Are We Going?" in Placher, pp. 338-339.

76   Amy B. Wang, "'Post-truth' named 2016 word of the year by Oxford Dictionaries." *The Washington Post,* www.washingtonpost.com/news/the-fix/wp/2016/11/16/post-truth-named-2016-word-of-the-year-by-oxford-dictionaries/?noredirect=on&utm_term=.a3162a107ab1, Nov 16, 2016.

77 Wang.

78 Norman L. Geisler and William D. *Watkins. Worlds Apart: A Handbook on World Views*. Wipf and Stock Publishers, 2003, p. 263.

79 McKee, p. 29.

80 Geisler and Watkins, p. 264.

81 Geisler and Watkins, p. 264.

82 Ravi Zacharias and Vince Vitale. *Jesus Among Secular Gods: The Countercultural Claims of Christ*. Faithwords, 2017, pp. 94-95.

83 Niebuhr, p. 2.

84 Niebuhr, p. 232.

85 Niebuhr, p. 2.

86 Niebuhr, p. 233.

87 C.S. Lewis, *Mere Christianity*. Harper One, 2015, pp. xv-xvi.

88 John Piper, "Does 'Mere Christianity' Mean Eliminate Denominations?" *Desiring God*. www.desiringgod.org/articles/does-mere-christianity-mean-eliminate-denominations, October 1, 2013.

89 *The Best Exotic Marigold Hotel*. Directed by John Madden, Fox Searchlight, 2011.

90 "The Nicene Creed." *The Christian Theology Reader*, 4th Ed., edited by in Alister E. McGrath, Wiley-Blackwell, 2011, p. 9.

For more information about

Finding Your Part in God's Master Story
and
Janet Ruth
please visit:

www.JaneTruth.com
www.GodsMasterStory.com
www.facebook.com/janetruthbooks
www.instagram.com/janetruthbooks

For more information about
AMBASSADOR INTERNATIONAL
please visit:

www.ambassador-international.com
@AmbassadorIntl
www.facebook.com/AmbassadorIntl

Thank you for reading this book. Please consider leaving us a
review on your social media, favorite retailer's website,
Goodreads or Bookbub, or our website.

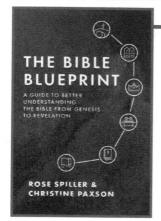

The Bible Blueprint divides the entire Bible chronologically into six easy to read parts. It provides a basic understanding of Scripture as a complete story that links all the various books together. It gives an overview of each book, touching on highlights and some of the amazing and significant events in each, without the reader getting bogged down in the more difficult sections.

In this powerful work, Dr. Wiles shares eighteen insights for learning how to pray, handle our anger, love our enemies, overcome worry, have a healthy marriage, and so much more. Included are questions for personal reflection or group discussions. *Don't Just Live . . . Really Live* offers a practical approach for discerning how to live out the Bible in today's world.

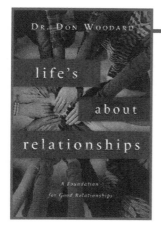

We interact with people every day whether it be with our coworkers, family, friends—life is filled with relationships! While not all relationships are good, with God's help, we can work to better our current and future relationships and overcome the effects of toxic relationships.

Made in the USA
Las Vegas, NV
19 January 2022

41820049R00090